To dear Ann, Michel and family,
With all our best Wishes.
Mahmoush, Nick
Samá & Bahyyieh
Aug 1995

BEHOLD ME

Behold Me

Bahá'í Writings on Unity

©1995 Bahá'í Publishing Trust
27 Rutland Gate
London SW7 1PD

All rights reserved

Based on a compilation originally prepared by George Allen

Photo Credits: Cover, pp 2, 8, 16, 22, 28, 40, 60, 70, Mark Howard/Twenty-Five Educational;
pp 38, 76, 90, 102, Steve Pyke/Network; p112, Liba Taylor/Select

British Library Cataloguing-in-Publication Data

A CIP catalogue record for this book is available from the British Library

ISBN 1 870989 59 7 cased
ISBN 1 870989 43 0 paper

♻ This book is printed on 100% recycled paper

'If any differences arise amongst you,
behold Me standing before your face,
and overlook the faults of one another
for My name's sake and as a token
of your love for My manifest
and resplendent Cause.'

Bahá'u'lláh

Contents

Note on sources   viii

Introduction   ix

1. The Oneness and Wholeness of the Human Race   1
2. 'O Contending Peoples of the Earth!'   7
3. The Universal Law of Attraction, Harmony and Unity   15
4. Overcoming Prejudices of Race and Colour   21
5. The Spirit of Oneness   27
6. Bahá'u'lláh, the Unifier   37
7. Unity Among Bahá'ís   49
8. The Role of the Bahá'í Community in Establishing World Unity   59
9. The Covenant; Axis of the Oneness of Humanity   69
10. Foundations of Unity   75
11. Individual Responsibility for Maintaining Unity Among Bahá'ís   89
12. Avoiding Backbiting, Fault-Finding and Criticism   101
13. 'Behold Me Standing Before Your Face …'   111

References   118

Index   123

Biographical notes   131

Further reading   132

Note on Sources

The written words of Bahá'u'lláh (1817-92), Founder of the Bahá'í Faith, and those of the Báb (1819-50), prophet-herald of the new religion, are regarded as the revealed Word of God, and are held sacred by Bahá'ís. These Writings are supplemented by the books, letters and published talks of 'Abdu'l-Bahá (1844-1921), eldest son of Bahá'u'lláh and appointed interpreter of His words.

The term, 'Bahá'í Writings', refers to all of these, plus letters written by, and on behalf of, Shoghi Effendi who was appointed Guardian of the Bahá'í Faith (1897-1957); and statements and letters written by, and on behalf of, the Universal House of Justice (first elected 1963).

The author and source of each passage are listed in the references section, page 118. Brief biographical notes on Bahá'u'lláh, the Báb, 'Abdu'l-Bahá, Shoghi Effendi and the Universal House of Justice can be found on page 131.

Introduction

As the new millennium approaches, we face our collective destiny as the human species. Beleaguered by war, poverty, pollution and disease, our shrinking world remains divided against itself, apparently unable to break free of the ideologies and lesser loyalties that promote injustice against the greater part of the world's population. A growing number of people, however, are confident that a new pattern of civilization is emerging from today's chaos. Firmly based on our recognition of the human race as one people, one family, it is a pattern which offers real hope for the future.

More than a hundred years ago, the prophet Bahá'u'lláh wrote that, 'The earth is but one country, and mankind its citizens.' For His followers – known as Bahá'ís – the unity of the human race is the next great step forward in our collective evolution, a process to which they dedicate their lives. This timely book shares a selection of the most important Bahá'í teachings on unity and reflects the experience and struggle of millions of people who have learned to see the earth as one common home.

Bahá'u'lláh's world-embracing vision is a source of inspiration to anyone who wishes to be free from narrow-minded provincialism, prejudice and fear. While proclaiming the need for a world order based on new standards of human rights and social and economic justice, and setting forth a code of laws and ethics to safeguard them, Bahá'u'lláh defines the great challenge of our age to be fundamentally spiritual in character. He demonstrates that love, compassion and forgiveness are still the most powerful remedies for conflict and contention between people, and that harmony and cooperation are the foundation of all human progress, not merely a consequence or by-product.

Such love flourishes when we disregard the incidental features of nationality, language, colour, class or creed, in favour of that inner spiritual reality we all share, the true source of human glory, dignity and happiness.

1

THE ONENESS AND WHOLENESS OF THE HUMAN RACE

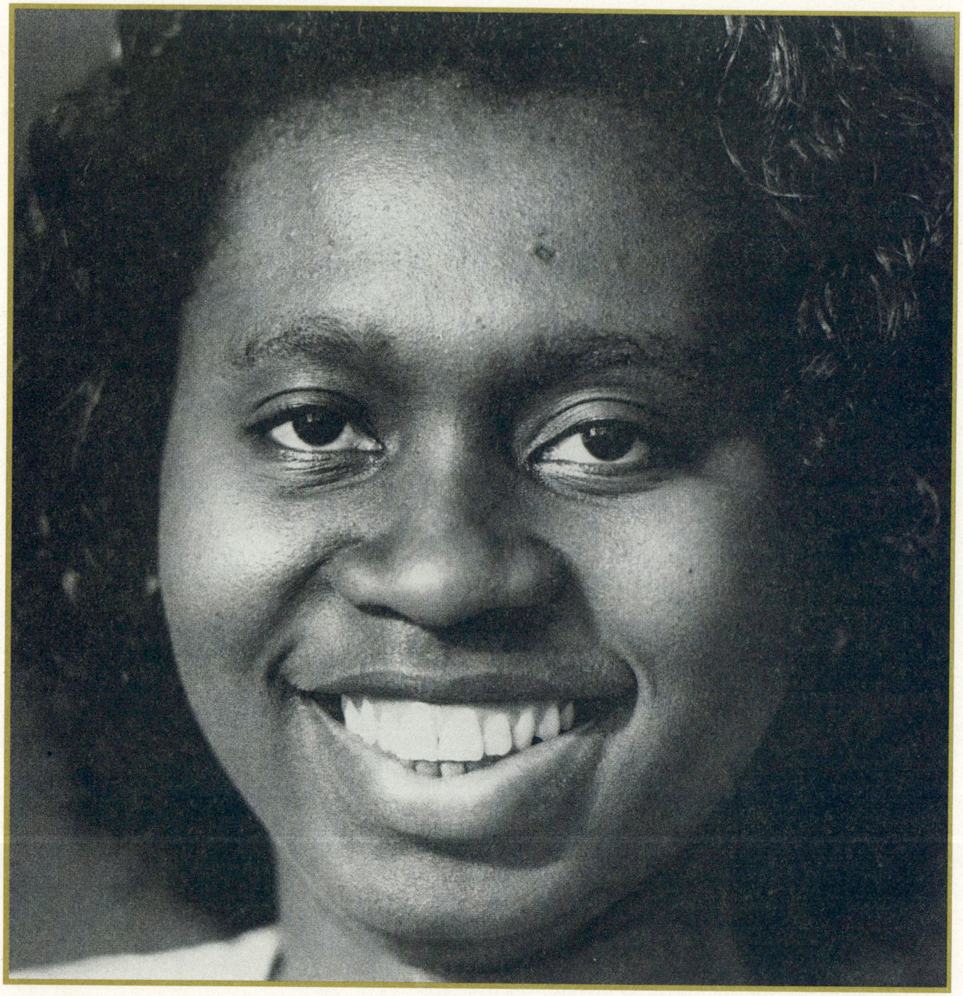

1   THE EARTH is but one country, and mankind its citizens.

2   THE INCOMPARABLE CREATOR hath created all men from one same substance…

3   THERE CAN BE NO DOUBT WHATEVER that the peoples of the world, of whatever race or religion, derive their inspiration from one heavenly Source, and are the subjects of one God.

4   LET NOT MAN GLORY in this that he loveth his country, let him rather glory in this that he loveth his kind.

5   GOD, THE ALMIGHTY, has created all mankind from the dust of earth. He has fashioned them all from the same elements; they are descended from the same race and live upon the same globe, He has created them to dwell beneath the one heaven. As members of the human family and His children He has endowed them with equal susceptibilities. He maintains, protects and is kind to all, He has made no distinction in mercies and graces among His children.

6   ALL MEN are the leaves and fruit of one same tree, they are all branches of the tree of Adam, they all have the same origin. The same rain has fallen upon them all, the same warm sun makes them grow, they are all refreshed by the same breeze. The only differences that exist and keep them apart are these: there are the children who need guidance, the ignorant to be instructed, the sick to be tended and healed…

7   THE GLORY of humanity is the heritage of each one.

There can be no doubt whatever that the peoples of the world, of whatever race or religion, derive their inspiration from one heavenly Source, and are the subjects of one God.

8   THIS EARTH is one home and native land. God has created mankind with equal endowment and right to live upon the earth.

9   IN THIS DAY . . . the five continents of the earth have virtually merged into one. And for everyone it is now easy to travel to any land, and to associate and exchange views with its peoples, and to become familiar, through publications, with the conditions, the religious beliefs and the thoughts of all men. In like manner all the members of the human family, whether peoples or governments, cities or villages, have become increasingly interdependent. For none is self-sufficiency any longer possible, inasmuch as political ties unite all peoples and nations, and the bonds of trade and industry, of agriculture and education, are being strengthened every day. Hence the unity of all mankind can in this day be achieved.

10   UNIFICATION of the whole of mankind is the hallmark of the stage which human society is now approaching. Unity of family, of tribe, of city-state, and nation have been successively attempted and fully established. World unity is the goal towards which a harassed humanity is striving. Nation-building has come to an end. The anarchy inherent in state sovereignty is moving towards a climax. A world, growing to maturity, must abandon this fetish, recognize the oneness and wholeness of human relationships, and establish once for all the machinery that can best incarnate this fundamental principle of its life.

11 WORLD ORDER can be founded only on an unshakeable consciousness of the oneness of mankind, a spiritual truth which all the human sciences confirm. Anthropology, physiology, psychology, recognize only one human species, albeit infinitely varied in the secondary aspects of life, Recognition of this truth requires abandonment of prejudice of every kind – race, class, colour, creed, nation, sex, degree of material civilization, everything which enables people to consider themselves superior to others.

12 AN URGE towards unity, like a spiritual springtime, struggles to express itself through countless international congresses that bring together people from a vast array of disciplines. It motivates appeals for international projects involving children and youth. Indeed, it is the real source of the remarkable movement toward ecumenism by which members of historically antagonistic religions and sects seem irresistibly drawn towards one another. Together with the opposing tendency to warfare and self-aggrandizement against which it ceaselessly struggles, the drive towards world unity is one of the dominant, pervasive features of life on the planet during the closing years of the twentieth century.

> *Together with the opposing tendency to warfare and self-aggrandizement against which it ceaselessly struggles, the drive towards world unity is one of the dominant, pervasive features of life on the planet during the closing years of the twentieth century.*

2

'O Contending Peoples and Kindreds of the Earth!'

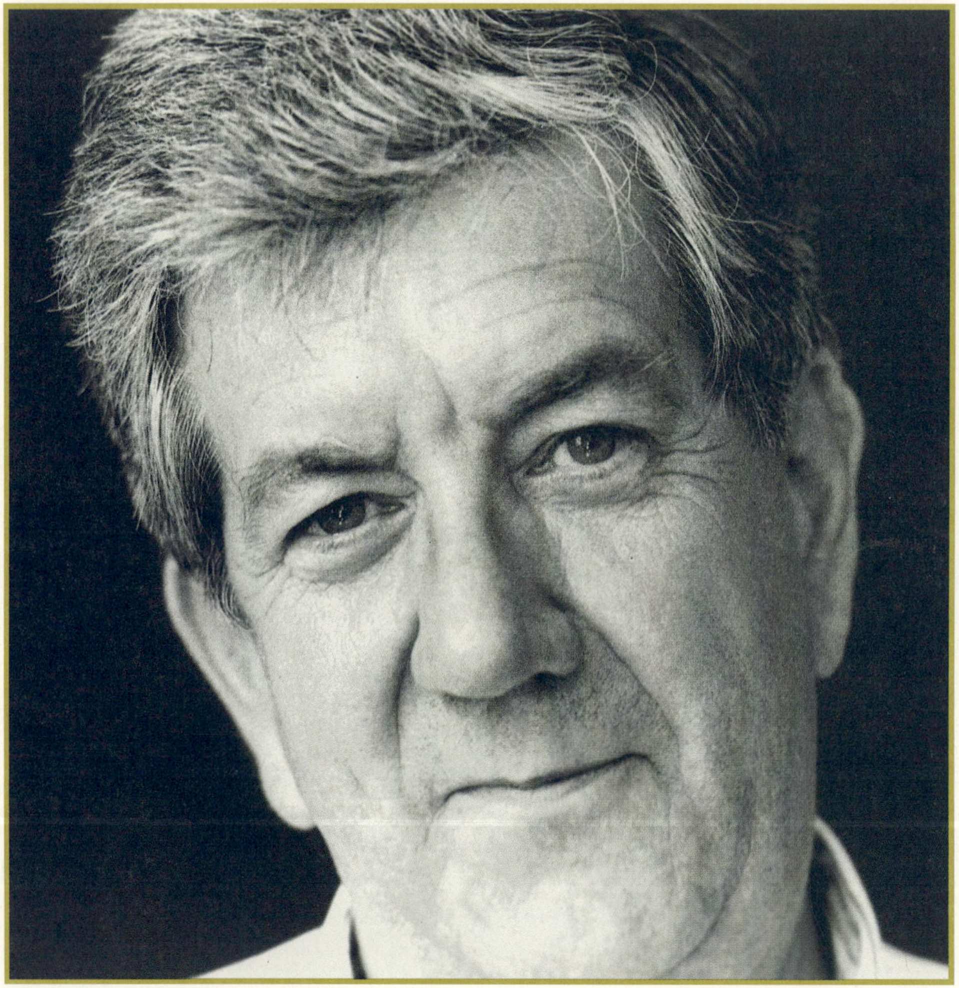

13 No power can exist except through unity.

14 So powerful is the light of unity that it can illuminate the whole earth.

15 O well-beloved ones! The tabernacle of unity hath been raised; regard ye not one another as strangers. Ye are the fruits of one tree, and the leaves of one branch.

16 It is permitted that the peoples and kindreds of the world associate with one another with joy and radiance. O people! Consort with the followers of all religions in a spirit of friendliness and fellowship.

17 No two men can be found who may be said to be outwardly and inwardly united. The evidences of discord and malice are apparent everywhere, though all were made for harmony and union.

18 Know ye not why We created you all from the same dust? That no one should exalt himself over the other. Ponder at all times in your hearts how ye were created. Since We have created you all from the same substance it is incumbent on you to be even as one soul, to walk with the same feet, eat with the same mouth and dwell in the same land, that from your inmost being, by your deeds and actions, the signs of oneness and the essence of detachment may be made manifest.

Ye are the fruits of one tree, and the leaves of one branch.

19 O CONTENDING PEOPLES and kindreds of the earth! Set your faces towards unity and let the radiance of its light shine upon you. Gather ye together, and for the sake of God resolve to root out whatever is the source of contention amongst you. Then will the effulgence of the world's great Luminary envelop the whole earth, and its inhabitants become the citizens of one city, and the occupants of one and the same throne.... Arise and, armed with the power of faith, shatter to pieces the gods of your vain imaginings, the sowers of dissension amongst you. Cleave unto that which draweth you together and uniteth you.

20 IT BEHOVETH the sovereigns of the world – may God assist them – or the ministers of the earth to take counsel together and to adopt one of the existing languages or a new one to be taught to children in schools throughout the world, and likewise one script. Thus the whole earth will come to be regarded as one country.

21 KNOW YE, verily, that the happiness of mankind lieth in the unity and the harmony of the human race, and that spiritual and material developments are conditioned upon love and amity among all men.

22 I CHARGE YOU ALL that each one of you concentrate all the thoughts of your heart on love and unity. When a thought of was comes, oppose it by a stronger thought of peace. A thought of hatred must be destroyed by a more powerful thought of love. Thoughts of war bring destruction to all harmony, well-being, restfulness and content.

    Thoughts of love are constructive of brotherhood, peace, friendship, and happiness.

23 THE EARTH has one surface. God has not divided this surface by boundaries and barriers to separate races and peoples. Man had set up and established these imaginary lines, giving to each restricted area a name and the limitation of a native land or nationhood. By this division and separation into groups and branches of mankind, prejudice is engendered which becomes a fruitful source of war and strife. Impelled by this prejudice, races and nations declare war against each other; the blood of the innocent is poured out, and the earth torn by violence. Therefore, it has been decreed by God in this day that these prejudices and differences shall be laid aside. All are commanded to seek the good pleasure of the Lord of unity, to follow His command and obey His will; in this way the world of humanity shall become illumined with the reality of love and reconciliation.

24 PREJUDICES OF ALL KINDS – whether religious, racial, patriotic or political – are destructive of divine foundations in man. All the warfare and bloodshed in human history have been the outcome of prejudice.

25 IN ORDER TO FIND TRUTH we must give up our prejudices, our own small trivial notions; an open receptive mind is essential. If our chalice is full of self, there is no room for the water of life. The fact that we imagine ourselves to be right and everybody else wrong is the greatest of all obstacles in the path towards unity, and unity is necessary if we are to reach truth, for truth is one.

Know ye, verily, that the happiness of mankind lieth in the unity and the harmony of the human race, and that spiritual and material developments are conditioned upon love and amity among all men.

26   IS IT NOT imagination and ignorance which impels man to violate the divine intention and make the very bounties of God the cause of war, bloodshed and destruction? Therefore, all prejudices between man and man are falsehoods and violations of the will of God. God desires unity and love; He commands harmony and fellowship. Enmity is human disobedience; God Himself is love.

27   DO NOT ALLOW difference of opinion, or diversity of thought to separate you from your fellowmen, or to be the cause of dispute, hatred and strife in your hearts.

    Rather, search diligently for the truth and make all men your friends.

28   THE WORLD IS, in truth, moving on towards its destiny. The interdependence of the peoples and nations of the earth, whatever the leaders of the divisive forces of the world may say or do, is already an accomplished fact. Its unity in the economic sphere is now understood and recognized. The welfare of the part means the welfare of the whole. The Revelation of Bahá'u'lláh has, in His own words, 'lent a fresh impulse and set a new direction' to this vast process now operating in the world. The fires lit by this great ordeal are the consequences of men's failure to recognize it. They are, moreover, hastening its consummation. Adversity, prolonged, worldwide, afflictive, allied to chaos and universal destruction, must needs convulse the nations, stir the conscience of the world, disillusion the masses, precipitate a radical change in the very conception of society, and coalesce ultimately the disjointed, the bleeding limbs of mankind into one body, single, organically united, and indivisible.

29   A WORLD FEDERAL SYSTEM, ruling the whole earth and exercising unchallengeable authority over its unimaginably vast resources, blending and embodying the ideals of both the East and the West, liberated from the curse of war and its miseries, and bent on the exploitation of all the available sources of energy on the surface of the planet, a system in which Force is made the servant of Justice, whose life is sustained by universal recognition of one God and by its allegiance to one common Revelation – such is the goal towards which humanity, impelled by the unifying forces of life, is moving.

30   THE EMERGENCE of a world community, the consciousness of world citizenship, the founding of a world civilization and culture – all of which must synchronize with the initial stages in the unfoldment of the Golden Age of the Bahá'í Era – should, by their very nature, be regarded, as far as this planetary life is concerned, as the furthermost limits in the organization of human society, though man, as an individual, will, nay must indeed as a result of such a consummation, continue indefinitely to progress and develop.

31   IN THE BAHÁ'Í VIEW, recognition of the oneness of mankind 'calls for no less than the reconstruction and the demilitarization of the whole civilized world – a world organically unified in all the essential aspects of its life, its political machinery, its spiritual aspiration, its trade and finance, its script and language, and yet infinite in the diversity of the national characteristics of its federated units.'

32   DISUNITY is a danger that the nations and peoples of the earth can no longer endure; the consequences are too terrible to contemplate, too obvious to require any demonstration.

> *In the Bahá'í view, recognition of the oneness of mankind 'calls for no less than the reconstruction and the demilitarization of the whole civilized world – a world organically unified in all the essential aspects of its life, its political machinery, its spiritual aspiration, its trade and finance, its script and language, and yet infinite in the diversity of the national characteristics of its federated units.'*

3

THE UNIVERSAL LAW OF ATTRACTION, HARMONY AND UNITY

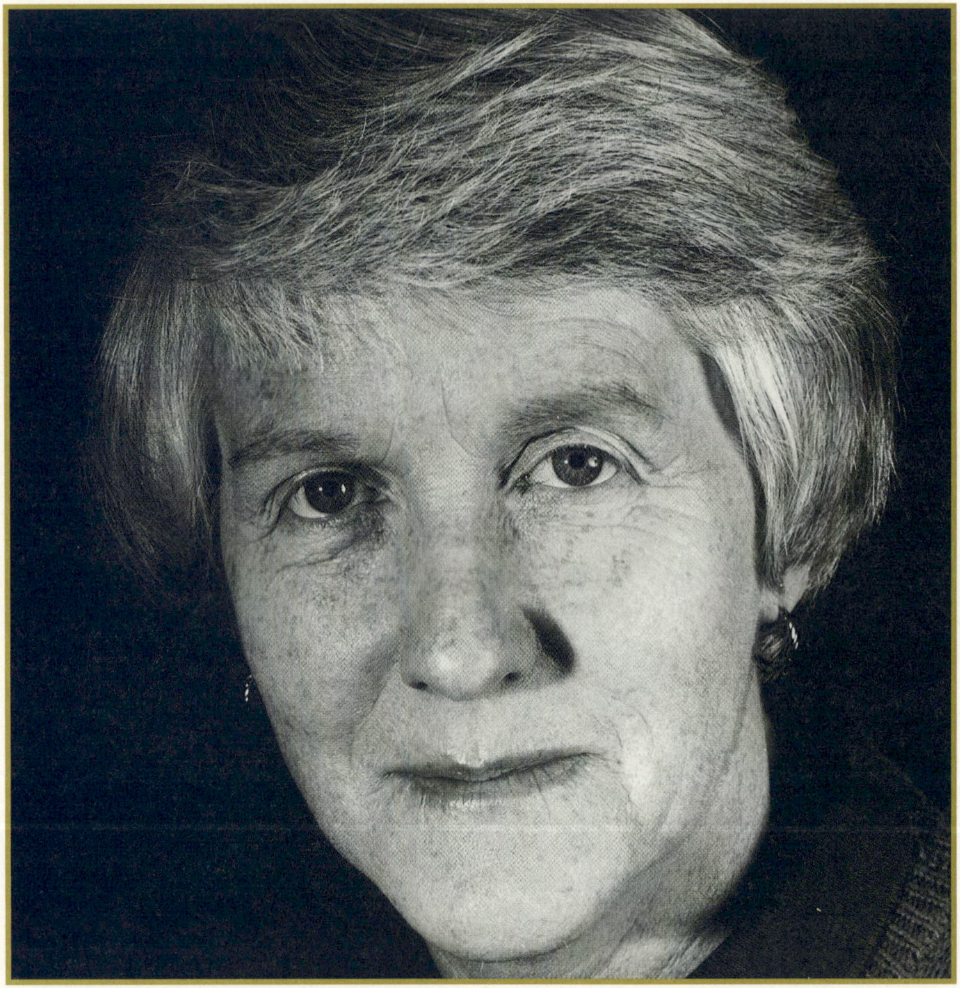

33 UNITY IS NECESSARY to existence. Love is the very cause of life; on the other hand, separation brings death. In the world of material creation, for instance, all things owe their actual life to unity. The elements which compose wood, mineral, or stone, are held together by the law of attraction. If this law should cease for one moment to operate these elements would not hold together, they would fall apart, and the object would in that particular form cease to exist… So it is with the great body of humanity. The wonderful Law of Attraction, Harmony and Unity, holds together this marvellous Creation.

34 LOOK ABOUT THEE at the world: here unity, mutual attraction, gathering together, engender life, but disunity and inharmony spell death. When thou dost consider all phenomena, thou wilt see that every created thing hath come into being through the mingling of many elements, and once this collectivity of elements is dissolved, and this harmony of components is dissevered, the life form is wiped out.

35 AS WITH THE WHOLE, so with the parts; whether a flower or a human body, when the attracting principle is withdrawn from it, the flower or the man dies. It is therefore clear that attraction, harmony, unity and love, are the cause of life, whereas repulsion, discord, hatred and separation bring death.

36 HUMAN BROTHERHOOD and dependence exist because mutual helpfulness and cooperation are the two necessary principles underlying human welfare. This is the physical relationship of mankind.

> *Human brotherhood and dependence exist because mutual helpfulness and cooperation are the two necessary principles underlying human welfare. This is the physical relationship of mankind.*

37 ❖ ❖ ❖ ALL PROGRESS is the result of association and cooperation, while ruin is the outcome of animosity and hatred.

38 ❖ ❖ ❖ THAT WHICH IS CONDUCIVE to association and attraction and unity among the sons of men is the means of the life of the world of humanity, and whatever causeth division, repulsion and remoteness leadeth to the death of humankind.

39 CONSIDER HOW NUMEROUS are these parts and members [of the human body], but the oneness of the animating sprit of life unites them all in perfect combination. It establishes such a unity in the bodily organism that if any part is subjected to injury or becomes diseased, all the other parts and functions sympathetically respond and suffer, owing to the perfect oneness existing.

40 REFLECT YE as to other than human forms of life and be ye admonished thereby: those clouds that drift apart cannot produce the bounty of the rain, and are soon lost; a flock of sheep, once scattered, falleth prey to the wolf, and birds that fly alone will be caught fast in the claws of the hawk. What greater demonstration could there be that unity leadeth to flourishing life, while dissension and withdrawing from the others, will lead only to misery; for these are the sure ways to disappointment and ruin.

41   ♦ ♦ ♦ IN THE WORLD of minds and souls, fellowship, which is an expression of composition, is conducive to life, whereas discord, which is an expression of decomposition, is the equivalent of death. Without cohesion among the individual elements which compose the body politic, disintegration and decay must inevitably follow and life be extinguished… Therefore, in the world of humanity it is wise and seemly that all the individual members should manifest unity and affinity. In the clustered jewels of the races may the blacks be as sapphires and rubies and the whites as diamonds and pearls. The composite beauty of humanity will be witnessed in their unity and blending. How glorious the spectacle of real unity among mankind! How conducive to peace, confidence and happiness if races and nations were united in fellowship and accord!

How glorious the spectacle of real unity among mankind! How conducive to peace, confidence and happiness if races and nations were united in fellowship and accord!

4

Overcoming Prejudices of Race and Colour

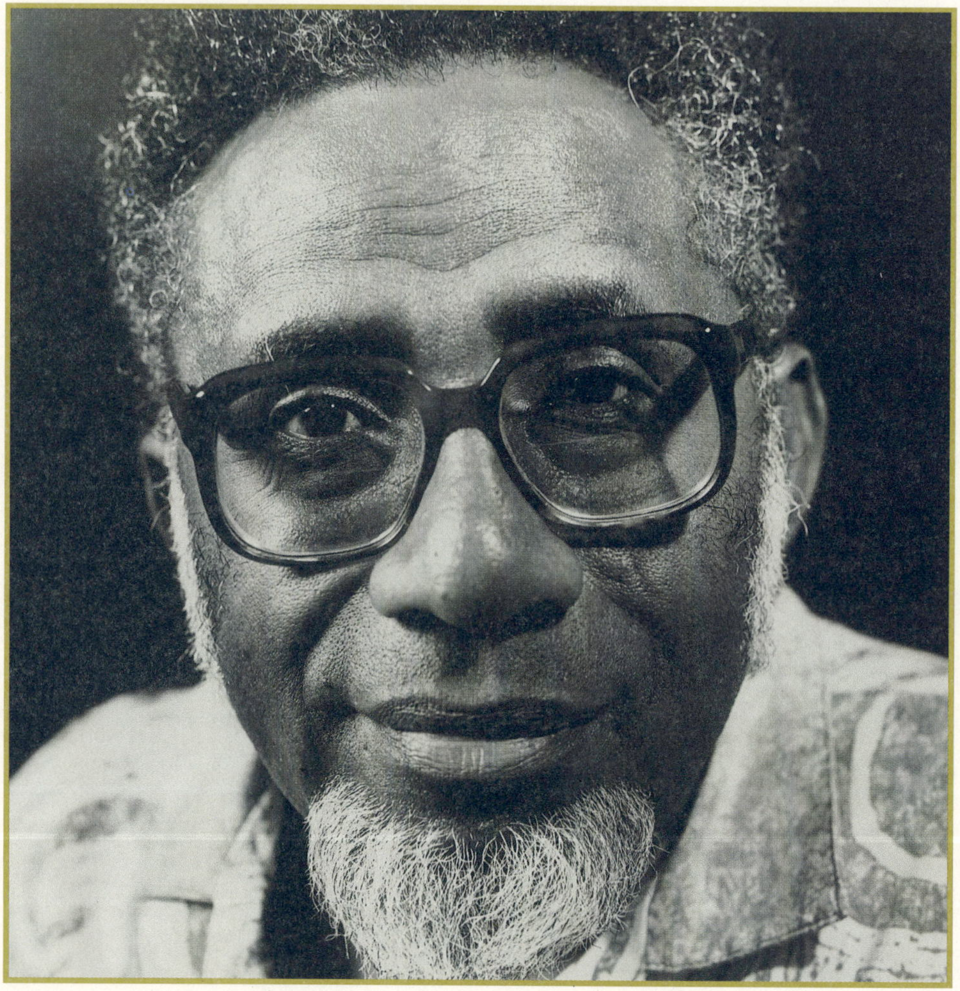

42   THERE IS NO GREATER MEANS to bring about affection between the white and the black than the influence of the Word of God.

43   YOU ALL ARE THE SERVANTS of one God and, therefore, brothers, sisters, mothers and fathers. In the sight of God there is no distinction between whites and blacks; all are one. Anyone whose heart is pure is dear to God – whether white or black, red or yellow.

44   GOD MAKETH NO DISTINCTION between the white and black. If the hearts are pure both are acceptable unto Him. God is no respecter of persons on account of either colour of race. All colours are acceptable unto Him, be they white, black or yellow. Inasmuch as we are all created in the image of God, we must bring ourselves to realize that all embody divine possibilities.

45   EXCELLENCE DOES NOT DEPEND on colour. Character is the true criterion of humanity. Anyone who possesses a good character, whose speech is good – that one is acceptable at the threshold of God no matter what colour he may be.

46   IN THE HUMAN KINGDOM ITSELF there are points of contact, properties common to all mankind; likewise there are points of distinction which separate race from race, individual from individual. If the points of contact, which are the common properties of humanity, overcome the peculiar points of distinction, unity is assured. On the other hand, if the points of differentiation overcome the points of agreement, disunion and weakness result. One of the important questions which affect the unity and the solidarity of mankind is the fellowship and equality of the white and coloured races. Between these two races certain points of agreement and points of distinction exist which warrant

> *God maketh no distinction between the white and black. If the hearts are pure both are acceptable unto Him. God is no respecter of persons on account of either colour of race.*

just and mutual consideration. The points of contact are many: for in the material or physical plane of being, both are constituted alike and exist under the same law of growth and bodily development. Furthermore, both live and move in the plane of the senses and are endowed with human intelligence. . . . In far numerous points of partnership and agreement exist between the two races: whereas the one point of distinction is that of colour. Shall this, the least of all distinctions, be allowed to separate you as races and individuals? In physical bodies, in the law of growth, in sense endowment, intelligence, patriotism, language, citizenship, civilization and religion you are one and the same. A single point of distinction exists – that of racial colour. God is not pleased with – neither should any reasonable or intelligent man be willing to recognize – inequality in the races because of this distinction. But there is need of a superior power to overcome human prejudices, a power which nothing in the world of mankind can withstand and which nothing in the world of mankind can withstand and which will overshadow the effect of all other forces at work in human conditions. That irresistible power is the love of God. It is my hope and prayer that it may destroy the prejudice of this one point of distinction between you and unite you all permanently under its hallowed protection.

47 CONCERNING THE PREJUDICE of race: it is an illusion, a superstition pure and simple! For God created us all of one race. There were no differences in the beginning, for we are all descendants of Adam. In the beginning, also, there were no limits and boundaries between the different lands; no part of the earth belonged more to one people than to another. In the sight of God there is no difference between the various races. Why should man invent such a prejudice? How can we uphold war caused by an illusion?

48 ♦♦♦ THE ENMITY AND HATRED which exist between the white and black races is very dangerous and there is no doubt that it will end in bloodshed unless the influence of the Word of God, the breaths of the Holy Spirit and the teachings of Bahá'u'lláh are diffused amongst them and harmony is established between the two races.

49 TO DISCRIMINATE against any race, on the ground of its being socially backward, politically immature, and numerically in a minority, is a flagrant violation of the spirit that animates the Faith of Bahá'u'lláh.

50 BOTH SIDES [whites and blacks] have prejudices to overcome; one, the prejudice which is built up in the minds of a people who have conquered and imposed their will, and the other the reactionary prejudice of those who have been conquered and sorely put upon.

51 RACISM, one of the most baneful and persistent evils, is a major barrier to peace. Its practice perpetrates too outrageous a violation of the dignity of human beings to be countenanced under any pretext. Racism retards the unfoldment of the boundless potentialities of its victims, corrupts its perpetrators, and blights human progress. Recognition of the oneness of mankind, implemented by appropriate legal measures, must be universally upheld if this problem is to be overcome.

> *To discriminate against any race, on the ground of its being socially backward, politically immature, and numerically in a minority, is a flagrant violation of the spirit that animates the Faith of Bahá'u'lláh.*

5

THE SPIRIT OF ONENESS

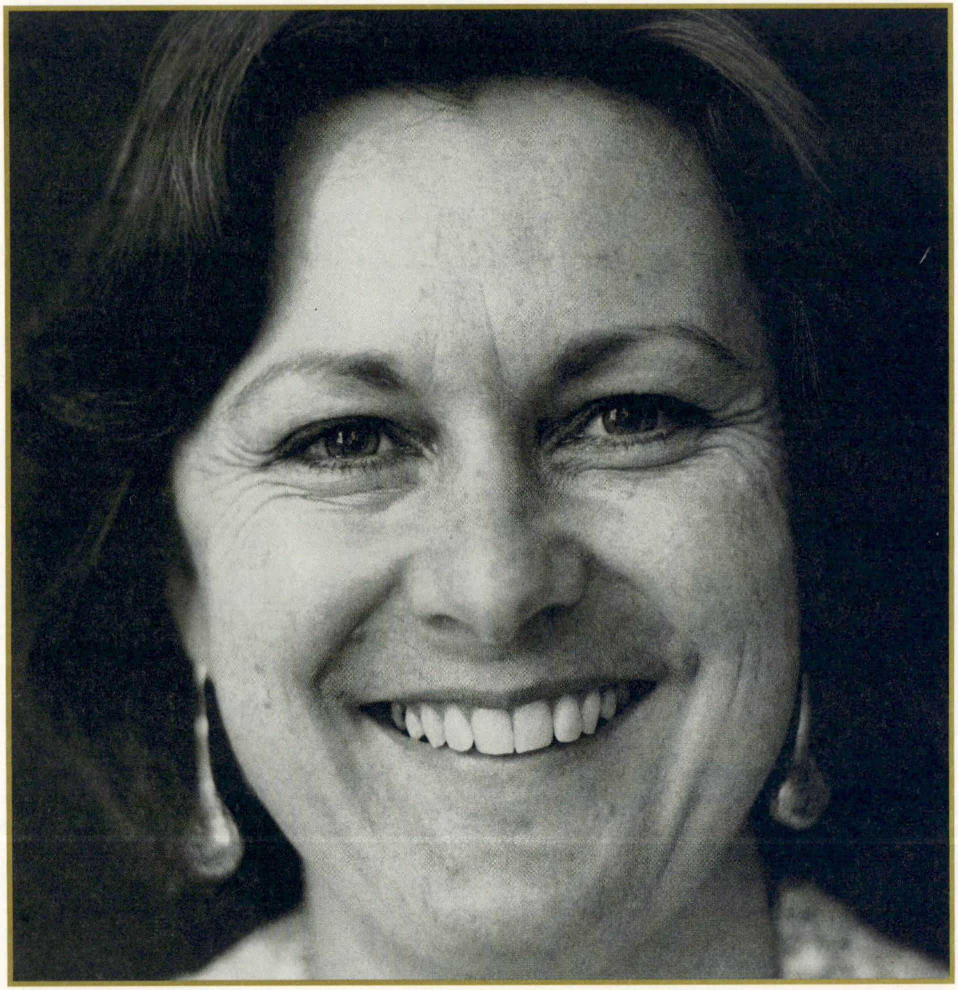

52 HE WHO IS YOUR LORD, the All-Merciful, cherisheth in His heart the desire of beholding the entire human race as one soul and one body.

53 THE PURPOSE OF RELIGION as revealed from the heaven of God's holy Will is to establish unity and concord amongst the peoples of the world; make it not the cause of dissension and strife. The religion of God and his divine law are the most potent instruments and the surest of all means for the dawning of the light of unity amongst men.

54 THE PROPHETS OF GOD should be regarded as physicians whose task is to foster the well-being of the world and its peoples, that, through the spirit of oneness, they may heal the sickness of a divided humanity.

55 THE DIVINE MESSENGERS have been sent down, and their Books were revealed, for the purpose of promoting the knowledge of God, and of furthering unity and fellowship amongst men.

56 RELIGION IS THE GREATEST of all means for the establishment of order in the world and the peaceful contentment of all that dwell therein.

57 ♦ ♦ ♦ IT IS EVIDENT that God has destined and intended religion to be the cause and means of cooperative effort and accomplishment among mankind. To this end He has sent the Prophets of God, the holy Manifestations of the Word, in order that the fundamental reality and religion of God may prove to be the bond of human unity, for the divine religions revealed by these holy Messengers have one and the same foundation. All will admit, therefore, that the divine religions are intended to be the

> *The purpose of religion as revealed from the heaven of God's holy Will is to establish unity and concord amongst the peoples of the world; make it not the cause of dissension and strife.*

means of true human cooperation, that they are united in the purpose of making humanity one family, for they rest upon the universal foundation of love, and love is the first effulgence of Divinity.

. . . The purpose of all the divine religions is the establishment of the bonds of love and fellowship among men.

58 THE GIFT OF GOD to this enlightened age is the knowledge of the oneness of mankind and of the fundamental oneness of religion. War shall cease between the nations, and by the will of God the Most Great Peace shall come; the world will be seen as a new world, and all men will live as brothers.

59 AND IN THIS NEW AND WONDROUS AGE, the Holy Writings say that we must be at one with every people; that we must see neither harshness nor injustice, neither malevolence, nor hostility, nor hate, but rather turn our eyes toward the heaven of ancient glory. For each of the creatures is a sign of God, and it was by the grace of the Lord and His power that each did step into the world; therefore they are not strangers, but in the family; not aliens, but friends, and to be treated as such.

60 CONSIDER THE FLOWERS of a garden: though differing in kind, colour, form and shape, yet, inasmuch as they are refreshed by the waters of one spring, revived by the breath of one wind, invigorated by the rays of one sun, this diversity increaseth their charm, and addeth unto their beauty. Thus when that unifying force, the penetrating influence of the Word of God, taketh effect, the difference of customs, manners, habits, ideas, opinions and dispositions embellisheth the world of humanity . . .

How unpleasing to the eye if all the flowers and plants, the leaves and blossoms, the fruits, the branches and the trees of that garden were all of the same shape and colour! Diversity of hues, form and shape, enricheth and adorneth the garden, and heighteneth the effect thereof. In like manner, when divers shades of thought, temperament and character, are brought under the power and influence of one central agency, the beauty and glory of human perfection will be revealed and made manifest.

61 NAUGHT BUT THE CELESTIAL POTENCY of the Word of God, which ruleth and transcendeth the realities of all things, is capable of harmonizing the divergent thoughts, sentiments, ideas, and convictions of the children of men. Verily, it is the penetrating power in all things, the mover of souls and the binder and regulator in the world of humanity.

62 WITH THE ADVENT of the Prophets of God, their power of creating a real union, one which is both external and of the heart, draws together malevolent peoples who have been thirsting for one another's blood, into the one shelter of the Word of God. Then a hundred thousand souls become as one soul, and unnumbered individuals emerge as one body.

63 MAN MUST CUT HIMSELF FREE from all prejudice and from the result of his own imagination, so that he may be able to search for truth unhindered. Truth is one in all religions, and by means of it the unity of the world can be realized.

> *The gift of God to this enlightened age is the knowledge of the oneness of mankind and of the fundamental oneness of religion.*

64   THE AGE HAS DAWNED when human fellowship will become a reality.

The century has come when all religions shall be unified.

The dispensation is at hand when all nations shall enjoy the blessings of international peace.

The cycle has arrived when racial prejudice will be abandoned by tribes and peoples of the world.

The epoch has begun wherein all native lands will be conjoined in one great human family.

For all mankind shall dwell in peace and security beneath the shelter of the great tabernacle of the one living God.

65   WHEN YOU LOVE a member of your family or a compatriot, let it be with a ray of the Infinite Love! Let it be in God, and for God! Wherever you find the attributes of God love that person, whether he be of your family or of another. Shed the light of a boundless love on every human being whom you meet, whether of your country, your race, your political party, or of any other nation, colour or shade of political opinion. Heaven will support you while you work in this ingathering of the scattered peoples of the world beneath the shadow of the almighty tent of unity.

66   BEING ONE, truth cannot be divided, and the differences that appear to exist among the nations only result from their attachment to prejudice. If only men would search out truth, they would find themselves united.

67   BAHÁ'U'LLÁH TEACHES that the world of humanity is in need of the breath of the Holy Spirit, for in spiritual quickening and enlightenment true oneness is attained with God and man.

68 THE REAL BROTHERHOOD is spiritual, for physical brotherhood is subject to separation. The wars of the outer world of existence separate humankind, but in the eternal world of spiritual brotherhood separation is unknown. Material or physical association is based upon earthly interests, but divine fellowship owes its existence to the breaths of the Holy Spirit.

69 SPIRITUAL BROTHERHOOD may be likened to the light, while the souls of humankind are as lanterns. The incandescent lamps here are many, yet the light is one.

70 THE HOLY SPIRIT is like unto the life in the human body, which blends all differences of parts and members in unity and agreement.

71 JUST AS THE HUMAN SPIRIT OF LIFE is the cause of coordination among the various parts of the human organism, the Holy Spirit is the controlling cause of the unity and coordination of mankind. That is to say, the bond or oneness of humanity cannot be effectively established save through the power of the Holy Spirit, for the world of humanity is a composite body, and the Holy Spirit is the animating principle of its life.

72 IT IS EVIDENT, therefore, that the foundation of real brotherhood, the cause of loving cooperation and reciprocity and the source of real kindness and unselfish devotion is none other than the breaths of the Holy Spirit. . . . When human brotherhood is founded upon the Holy Spirit, it is eternal, changeless, unlimited.

> *Being one, truth cannot be divided, and the differences that appear to exist among the nations only result from their attachment to prejudice. If only men would search out truth, they would find themselves united.*

73   It is certain that the greatest of instrumentalities for achieving the advancement and the glory of man, the supreme agency for the enlightenment and the redemption of the world, is love and fellowship and unity among all the members of the human race. Nothing can be effected in the world, not even conceivably, without unity and agreement, and the perfect means for engendering fellowship and union is true religion.

74   The Divine Manifestations since the day of Adam have striven to unite humanity so that all may be accounted as one soul. The function and purpose of a shepherd is to gather and not disperse his flock. The Prophets of God have been divine Shepherds of humanity. They have established a bond of love and unity among mankind, made scattered peoples one nation and wandering tribes a mighty kingdom. They have laid the foundation of the oneness of God and summoned all to universal peace.

75   ♦ ♦ ♦ The Lord of mankind has caused His holy, divine Manifestations to come into the world. He has revealed His heavenly Books in order to establish spiritual brotherhood and through the power of the Holy Spirit has made it practicable for perfect fraternity to be realized among mankind. And when through the breaths of the Holy Spirit this perfect fraternity and agreement are established amongst men – this brotherhood and love being spiritual in character, this loving kindness being heavenly, these constraining bonds being divine – a unity appears which is indissoluble, unchanging and never subject to transformation. It is ever the same and will forever remain the same.

76 FOR A SINGLE PURPOSE were the Prophets, each and all, sent down to earth; for this was Christ made manifest, for this did Bahá'u'lláh raise up the call of the Lord: that the world of man should become the world of God, this nether realm the Kingdom, this darkness light, this satanic wickedness all the virtues of heaven – and unity, fellowship and love be won for the whole human race, that the organic unity should reappear and the bases of discord be destroyed and life everlasting and grace everlasting become the harvest of mankind.

77 I HOPE THAT THE LIGHTS of the Sun of Reality will illumine the whole world so that no strife and warfare, no battles and bloodshed remain. May fanaticism and religious bigotry be unknown, all humanity enter the bond of brotherhood, souls consort in perfect agreement, the nations of earth at last hoist the banner of truth and the religions of the world enter the divine temple of oneness, for the foundation of the heavenly religions are one reality. Reality is not divisible; it does not admit multiplicity. All the holy Manifestations of God have proclaimed and promulgated the same reality. They have summoned mankind to reality itself and reality is one. The clouds and mists of imitations have obscured the Sun of Truth. We must forsake these imitations, dispel these clouds and mists and free the Sun from the darkness of superstition. Then will the Sun of Truth shine most gloriously; then all the inhabitants of the world will be united, the religions will be one, sects and denominations will reconcile, all nationalities will flow together in the recognition of one Fatherhood and all degrees of humankind gather in the shelter of the same tabernacle, under the same banner.

> *Nothing can be effected in the world, not even conceivably, without unity and agreement, and the perfect means for engendering fellowship and union is true religion.*

78   IT IS MY HOPE . . . that these many rivers, each flowing along in diverse and separated beds, will find their way back to the circumambient sea, and merge together and rise up in a single wave of surging oneness; that the unity of truth, through the power of God, will make these illusory differences to vanish away. This is the one essential: for if unity be gained, all other problems will disappear of themselves.

79   THE DIFFERENCES among the religions of the world are due to the varying types of minds. So long as the powers of the mind are various, it is certain that men's judgements and opinions will differ one from another. If, however, one single, universal perceptive power be introduced – a power encompassing all the rest – those differing opinions will merge, and a spiritual harmony and oneness will become apparent.

80   THEY WHOSE HEARTS ARE WARMED by the energizing influence of God's creative love cherish His creatures for His sake, and recognize in every human face a sign of His reflected glory.

6

Bahá'u'lláh, the Unifier

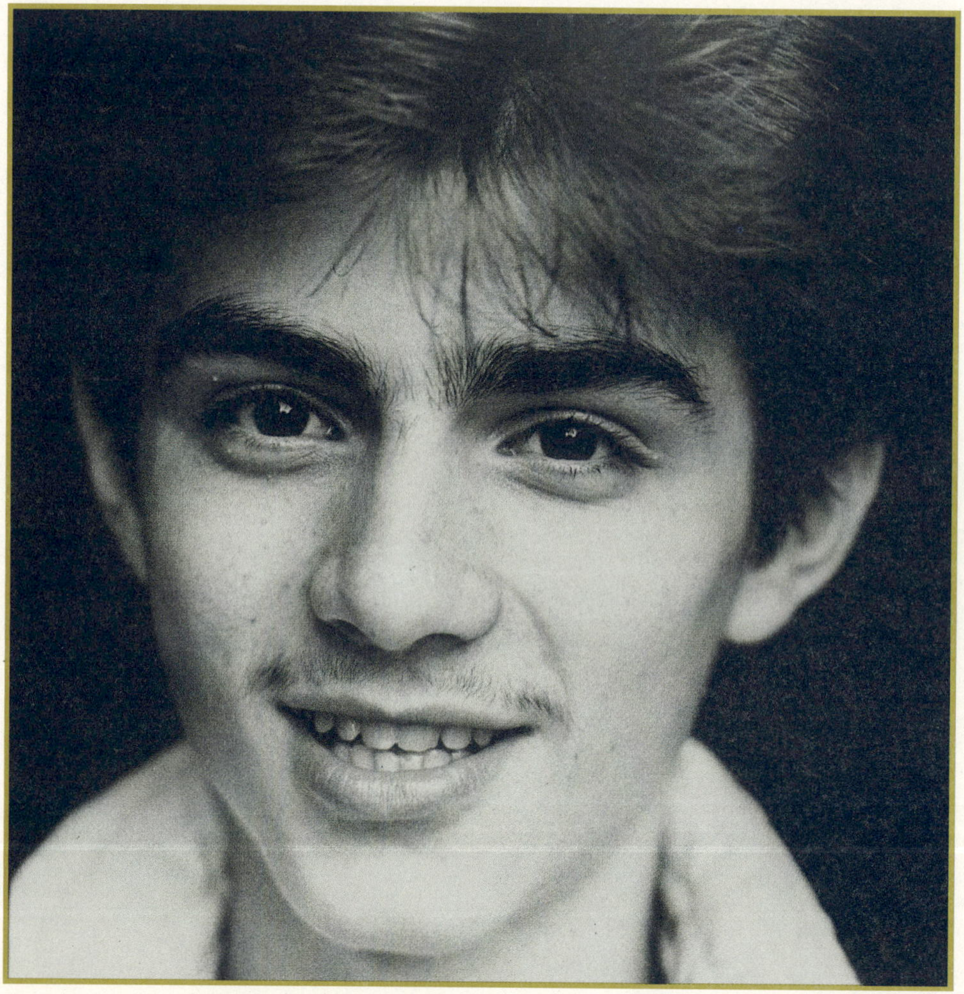

81 T̲HAT WHICH GOD HATH ORDAINED as the sovereign remedy and mightiest instrument for the healing of the world is the union of all its peoples in one universal Cause, one common Faith. This can in no wise be achieved except through the power of a skilled, an all-powerful, and inspired Physician.

82 THE WELL-BEING of mankind, its peace and security, are unattainable unless and until its unity is firmly established. This unity can never be achieved so long as the counsels which the Pen of the Most High hath revealed are suffered to pass unheeded. Through the power of the words He hath uttered the whole of the human race can be illumined with the light of unity, and the remembrance of His Name is able to set on fire the hearts of all men, and burn away the veils that intervene between them and His glory.

83 O YE THAT DWELL on earth! The distinguishing feature that marketh the preeminent character of this Supreme Revelation consisteth in that We have, on the one hand, blotted out from the pages of God's holy Book whatsoever hath been the cause of strife, of malice and mischief amongst the children of men, and have, on the other, laid down the essential prerequisites of concord, of understanding, of complete and enduring unity. Well is it with them that keep My statutes.

84 THIS IS THE DAY in which God's most excellent favours have been poured out upon men, the Day in which His most mighty grace hath been infused into all created things. It is incumbent upon all the peoples of the world to reconcile their differences, and, with perfect unity and peace, abide beneath the shadow of the Tree of His care and loving kindness.

> *The well-being of mankind, its peace and security, are unattainable unless and until its unity is firmly established. This unity can never be achieved so long as the counsels which the Pen of the Most High hath revealed are suffered to pass unheeded.*

85   Through each and every one of the verses which the Pen of the Most High hath revealed, the doors of love and unity have been unlocked and flung open to the face of men. We have erewhile declared – and Our Word is the truth – :'Consort with the followers of all religions in a spirit of friendliness and fellowship.' Whatsoever hath led the children of men to shun one another, and hath caused dissensions and divisions amongst them, hath, through the revelation of these words, been nullified and abolished.

86   Revile ye not one another. We, verily, have come to unite and weld together all that dwell on earth. Unto this beareth witness what the ocean of Mine utterance hath revealed amongst men, and yet most of the people have gone astray. If anyone revile you, or trouble touch you, in the path of God, be patient, and put your trust in Him Who heareth, Who seeth. He, in truth, witnesseth, and perceiveth, and doeth what He pleaseth, through the power of His sovereignty. He, verily, is the Lord of strength, and of might. In the Book of God, the Mighty, the Great, ye have been forbidden to engage in contention and conflict. Lay fast hold on whatever will profit you, and profit the peoples of the world.

87   Bahá'u'lláh has drawn the circle of unity, He has made a design for the uniting of all the peoples, and for the gathering of them all under the shelter of the tent of universal unity. This is the work of the Divine Bounty, and we must all strive with heart and soul until we have the reality of unity in our midst, and as we work, so will strength be given unto us.

88 At a time when warfare and strife prevailed among nations, when enmity and hatred separated sects and denominations and human differences were very great, Bahá'u'lláh appeared upon the horizon of the East, proclaiming the oneness of God and the unity of the world of humanity. He promulgated the teaching that all mankind are the servants of one God; that all have come into being through the bestowal of the one Creator; that God is kind to all, nurtures, rears and protects all, provides for all and extends His love and mercy to all races and people.

89 Now Bahá'u'lláh has proclaimed the 'Unity of the World of Mankind'. All peoples and nations are of one family, the children of one Father, and should be to one another as brothers and sisters! I hope that you will endeavour in your lives to show forth and spread this teaching. Bahá'u'lláh said that we should love even our enemies and be to them as friends. If all men were obedient to this principle, the greatest unity and understanding would be established in the hearts of mankind.

90 ♦ ♦ ♦ In all religious teachings of the past, the human world has been represented as divided into two parts, one known as the people of the Book of God or the pure tree and the other the people of infidelity and error or the evil tree. The former were considered as belonging to the faithful and the others to the hosts of the irreligious and infidel; one part of humanity the recipients of divine mercy and the other the object of the wrath of their Creator . . . Bahá'u'lláh removed this by proclaiming the oneness of the world of humanity.

> *Bahá'u'lláh has drawn the circle of unity, He has made a design for the uniting of all the peoples, and for the gathering of them all under the shelter of the tent of universal unity.*

91 IN THIS SACRED DISPENSATION, conflict and contention are in no wise permitted. Every aggressor deprives himself of God's grace. It is incumbent upon everyone to show the utmost love, rectitude of conduct, straightforwardness and sincere kindliness unto all the peoples and kindreds of the world, be they friends or strangers. So intense must be the spirit of love and loving kindness, that the stranger may find himself a friend, the enemy a true brother, no difference whatsoever existing between them. For universality is of God and all limitations earthly.

92 IN THIS WONDROUS AGE, at this time when the Ancient Beauty, the Most Great Name, bearing unnumbered gifts, hath risen above the horizon of the world, the Word of God hath infused such awesome power into the inmost essence of humankind that He hath stripped men's human qualities of all effect, and hath, with His all-conquering might, unified the peoples in a vast sea of oneness.

93 SO INTENSELY hath the glory of Divine Unity penetrated souls and hearts that all are now bound one to another with heavenly ties, and all are even as a single heart, a single soul. Wherefore reflections of the spirit and impressions of the Divine are now mirrored clear and sharp in the deep heart's core. I beg of God to strengthen these spiritual bonds as day followeth day, and make this mystic oneness to shine ever more brightly, until at last all shall be as troops marshalled together beneath the banner of the Covenant within the sheltering shade of the Word of God; that they may strive with all their might until universal fellowship, close and warm, and unalloyed love, and spiritual relationships, will connect all the hearts in the world. Then will all humankind, because of this fresh and dazzling bounty, be gathered in a single

homeland. Then will conflict and dissension vanish from the face of the earth, then will mankind be cradled in love for the beauty of the All-glorious. Discord will change to accord, dissension to unison. The roots of malevolence will be torn out, the basis of aggression destroyed. The bright rays of union will obliterate the darkness of limitations, and the splendours of heaven will make the human heart to be even as a mine veined richly with the love of God.

94 Let there be no misgivings as to the animating purpose of the world-wide Law of Bahá'u'lláh. Far from aiming at the subversion of the existing foundations of society, it seeks to broaden its basis, to remould its institutions in a manner consonant with the needs of an ever-changing world. It can conflict with no legitimate allegiances, nor can it undermine essential loyalties. Its purpose is neither to stifle the flame of a sane and intelligent patriotism in men's hearts, nor to abolish the system of national autonomy so essential if the evils of excessive centralization are to be avoided. It does not ignore, nor does it attempt to suppress, the diversity of ethnical origins, of climate, of history, of language and tradition, of thought and habit, that differentiate the peoples and nations of the world. It calls for a wider loyalty, for a larger aspiration than any that has animated the human race. It insists upon the subordination of national impulses and interests to the imperative claims of a unified world. It repudiates excessive centralization on one hand, and disclaims all attempts at uniformity on the other. Its watchword is unity in diversity . . .

Every aggressor deprives himself of God's grace. It is incumbent upon everyone to show the utmost love, rectitude of conduct, straightforwardness and sincere kindliness unto all the peoples and kindreds of the world, be they friends or strangers.

95 THE PRINCIPLE of the Oneness of Mankind – the pivot around which all the teachings of Bahá'u'lláh revolve – is no mere outburst of ignorant emotionalism or an expression of vague and pious hope. Its appeal is not to be merely identified with a re-awakening of the spirit of brotherhood and goodwill among men, nor does it aim solely at the fostering of harmonious co-operation among individual peoples and nations. Its implications are deeper, its claims greater than any which the prophets of old were allowed to advance. Its message is applicable not only to the individual, but concerns itself primarily with the nature of those essential relationships that must bind all the states and nations as members of one family. . . . It implies an organic change in the structure of present-day society, a change such as the world has not yet experienced. . . . It calls for no less than the reconstruction and demilitarization of the whole civilized world – a world organically unified in all the essential aspects of its life, its political machinery, its spiritual aspiration, its trade and finance, its script and language, and yet infinite in the diversity of the national characteristics of its federated units.

96 THE PRINCIPLE of the Oneness of Mankind, as proclaimed by Bahá'u'lláh, carries with it no more and no less than a solemn assertion that attainment to this final stage in this stupendous evolution is not only necessary but inevitable, that its realization is fast approaching, and that nothing short of a power that is born of God can succeed in establishing it.

97 THE WHOLE OF MANKIND is groaning, is dying to be led to unity, and to terminate its age-long martyrdom. And yet it stubbornly refuses to embrace the light and acknowledge the sovereign authority of the one Power that can extricate it from its entanglements, and avert the woeful calamity that threatens to engulf it.

98 THE UNITY OF THE HUMAN RACE, as envisaged by Bahá'u'lláh, implies the establishment of a world commonwealth in which all nations, races, creeds and classes are closely and permanently united, and in which the autonomy of its state members and the personal freedom and initiative of the individuals that compose them are definitely and completely safeguarded.

99 THE FUNDAMENTAL PURPOSE of the Faith of Bahá'u'lláh is the realization of the organic unity of the entire human race.

100 WHEN BAHÁ'U'LLÁH PROCLAIMED His Message to the world in the nineteenth century He made it abundantly clear that the first step essential for the peace and progress of mankind was its unification. As He says, 'The well-being of mankind, its peace and security are unattainable unless and until its unity is firmly established.' To this day, however, you will find most people take the opposite view: they look upon unity as an ultimate, almost unattainable goal and concentrate first on remedying all the other ills of mankind. If they did but know it, these other ills are but various symptoms of the basic disease – disunity.

> *When Bahá'u'lláh proclaimed His Message to the world in the nineteenth century He made it abundantly clear that the first step essential for the peace and progress of mankind was its unification.*

101 From the beginning of His stupendous mission, Bahá'u'lláh urged upon the attention of nations the necessity of ordering human affairs in such a way as to bring into being a world unified in all the essential aspects of its life. In unnumbered verses and Tablets He repeatedly and variously declared the 'progress of the world' and the 'development of the nations' as being among the ordinances of God for this day. The oneness of mankind, which is at once the operating principle and ultimate goal of His Revelation, implies the achievement of a dynamic coherence between the spiritual and practical requirements of life on earth.

102 How noteworthy that in the Order of Bahá'u'lláh, while the individual will is subordinated to that of society, the individual is not lost in the mass but becomes the focus of primary development, so that he may find his own place in the flow of progress, and society as a whole may benefit from the accumulated talents and abilities of the individuals composing it. Such an individual finds fulfilment of his potential not merely in satisfying his own wants but in realizing his completeness in being at one with humanity and with the divinely ordained purpose of creation.

103 The spirit of liberty which recent decades has swept over the planet with such tempestuous force is a manifestation of the vibrancy of the Revelation brought by Bahá'u'lláh. His own words confirm it. 'The Ancient Beauty,' He wrote in a soul-stirring commentary on His sufferings, 'hath consented to be bound with chains that mankind may be freed from its bondage, and hath accepted to be made a prisoner within this most mighty Stronghold that the whole world may attain unto true liberty.'

Might it not be reasonably concluded then, that 'true liberty' is His gift of love to the human race? Consider what Bahá'u'lláh has done: He revealed laws and principles to guide the free; He established an Order to channel the actions of the free; He proclaimed a Covenant to guarantee the unity of the free.

Thus, we hold to this ultimate perspective: Bahá'u'lláh came to set humanity free. His Revelation is, indeed, an invitation to freedom – freedom from want, freedom from war, freedom to unite, freedom to progress, freedom in peace and joy.

Bahá'u'lláh came to set humanity free. His Revelation is, indeed, an invitation to freedom – freedom from want, freedom from war, freedom to unite, freedom to progress, freedom in peace and joy.

7

Unity Among Bahá'ís

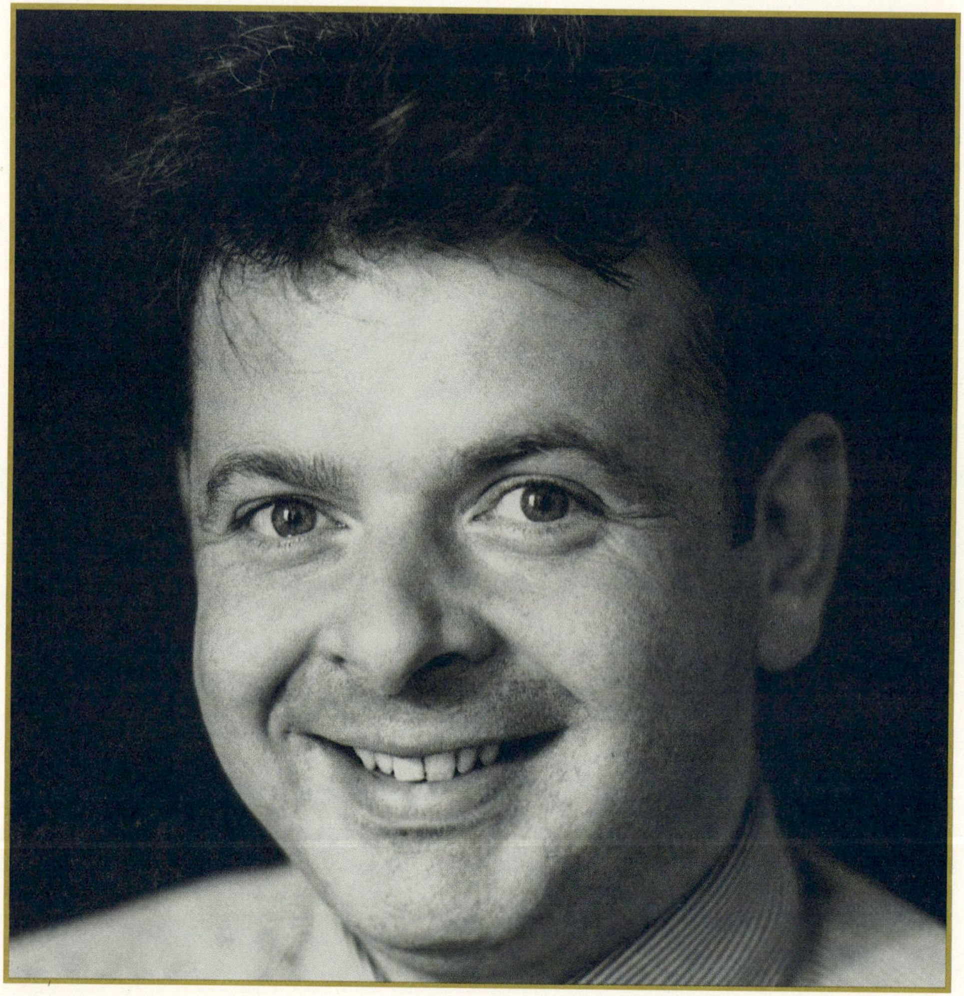

104   T̲he fundamental purpose animating the Faith of God and His Religion is to safeguard the interests and promote the unity of the human race, and to foster the spirit of love and fellowship amongst men. Suffer it not to become a source of dissension and discord, of hate and enmity.

105   After man's recognition of God, and becoming steadfast in His Cause the station of affection, of harmony, of concord and of unity is superior to that of most other goodly deeds.

106   O people of Bahá! Ye are the dawning-places of the love of God and the daysprings of His loving-kindness. Defile not your tongues with the cursing and reviling of any soul, and guard your eyes against that which is not seemly. . . . Ye are all the leaves of one tree and the drops of one ocean.

107   O friends! Be not careless of the virtues with which ye have been endowed, neither be neglectful of your high destiny. Suffer not your labours to be wasted through the vain imaginations which certain hearts have devised. Ye are the stars of the heaven of understanding, the breeze that stirreth at the break of day, the soft-flowing waters upon which must depend the very life of all men, the letters inscribed upon His sacred scroll. With the utmost unity, and in a spirit of perfect fellowship, exert yourselves, that ye may be enabled to achieve that which beseemeth this Day of God. Verily I say, strife and dissension, and whatsoever the mind of man abhorreth are entirely unworthy of his station. Centre your energies in the propagation of the Faith of God.

> *The fundamental purpose animating the Faith of God and His Religion is to safeguard the interests and promote the unity of the human race, and to foster the spirit of love and fellowship amongst men.*

108   T<small>HIS WRONGED ONE</small> hath forbidden the people of God to engage in contention or conflict and hath exhorted them to righteous deeds and praiseworthy character.

109   L<small>ET NOT THE MEANS</small> of order be made the cause of confusion and the instrument of union an occasion for discord. We fain would hope that the people of Bahá may be guided by the blessed words: 'Say: all things are of God.' This exalted utterance is like unto water for quenching the fire of hate and enmity which smouldereth within the hearts and breasts of men.

110   E<small>VER SINCE THE SEEKING</small> of preference and distinction came into play, the world hath been laid waste. It hath become desolate. Those who have quaffed from the ocean of divine utterance and fixed their gaze upon the Realm of Glory should regard themselves as being on the same level as the others and in the same station. Were this matter to be definitely established and conclusively demonstrated through the power and might of God, the world would become as the Abhá Paradise. Indeed, man is noble, inasmuch as each one is a repository of the sign of God. Nevertheless, to regard oneself as superior in knowledge, learning or virtue, or to exalt oneself or seek preference, is a grievous transgression. Great is the blessedness of those who are adorned with the ornament of this unity and have been graciously confirmed by God.

111   W<small>E HAVE CREATED YOU</small> from one tree and have caused you to be as the leaves and fruit of the same tree, that haply ye may become a source of comfort to one another. Regard ye not others save as ye regard your own selves, that no feeling of aversion may prevail amongst you.

112 BECOME AS TRUE BRETHREN in the one and indivisible religion of God, free from distinction, for verily God desireth that your hearts should become mirrors unto your brethren in the Faith, so that ye find yourselves reflected in them, and they in you.

113 THE LOVE WHICH EXISTS between the hearts of believers is prompted by the ideal of the unity of spirits. This love is attained through the knowledge of God, so that men see the divine love reflected in the heart. Each sees in the other the beauty of God reflected in the soul, and finding this point of similarity, they are attracted to one another in love. This love will make all men the waves of one sea, this love will make them all the stars of one heaven and the fruits of one tree. This love will bring the realization of true accord, the foundation of real unity.

114 THE GREAT AND FUNDAMENTAL TEACHINGS of Bahá'u'lláh are the oneness of God and unity of mankind. This is the bond of union among Bahá'ís all over the world. They become united among themselves, then unite others. . . . Now must we, likewise, bind ourselves together in the utmost unity, be kind and loving to each other, sacrificing all our possessions, our honour, yea, even our lives for each other. Then will it be proved that we have acted according to the teachings of God, that we have been real believers in the oneness of God and unity of mankind.

115 I DESIRE DISTINCTION for you. The Bahá'ís must be distinguished from others of humanity. But this distinction must not depend upon wealth – that they should become more affluent than other people. I do not desire for you financial distinction. It is not an ordinary distinction I desire; not scientific, commercial, industrial distinction. For you I desire spiritual distinction – that is, you must

> *The great and fundamental teachings of Bahá'u'lláh are the oneness of God and unity of mankind. This is the bond of union among Bahá'ís all over the world. They become united among themselves, then unite others.*

become eminent and distinguished in morals. In the love of God you must become distinguished from all else. You must become distinguished for loving humanity, for unity and accord, for love and justice. In brief, you must become distinguished in all the virtues of the human world – for faithfulness and sincerity, for justice and fidelity, for firmness and steadfastness, for philanthropic deeds and service to the human world, for love toward every human being, for unity and accord with all people, for removing prejudices and promoting international peace.

116 THE AIM OF THE APPEARANCE of the Blessed Perfection – may my life be a sacrifice for His beloved ones! – was the unity and agreement of all the people of the world. Therefore, my utmost desire, firstly, is the accord and union and love of the believers and after that of all the people of the world. Now, if unity and agreement is not established among the believers, I will become heartbroken and the afflictions will leave a greater imprint upon me. But if the fragrance of love and unity among the believers is wafted to my nostrils, every trial will become a mercy, every unhappiness a joy, every difficulty an expansion, every misery a treasure and every hardship a felicity.

117 WHEREFORE MUST the friends of God, with utter sanctity, with one accord, rise up in the spirit, in unity with one another, to such a degree that they will become even as one being and one soul. On such a plane as this, physical bodies play no part, rather doth the spirit take over and rule; and when its power encompasseth all then is spiritual union achieved.

118 STRIVE YE BY DAY AND NIGHT to cultivate your unity to the fullest degree. Let your thoughts dwell on your own spiritual development, and close your eyes to the deficiencies of other souls. Act ye in such wise, showing forth pure and goodly deeds, and modesty and humility, that ye will cause others to be awakened.

119 WHEREFORE, O ye beloved of the Lord, bestir yourselves, do all in your power to be as one, to live in peace, each with the others: for ye are all the drops from but one ocean, the foliage of one tree, the pearls from a single shell, the flowers and sweet herbs from the same one garden. And achieving that, strive ye to unite the hearts of those who follow other faiths.

120 BECOME AS WAVES of one sea, trees of one forest, growing in the utmost love, agreement and unity.

If you attain to such a capacity of love and unity, the Blessed Perfection will shower infinite graces of the spiritual Kingdom upon you, guide, protect and preserve you under the shadow of His Word, increase your happiness in this world and uphold you through all difficulties.

121 TODAY THE ONE OVERRIDING NEED is unity and harmony among the beloved of the Lord, for they should have among them but one heart and soul . . . they must bring to an end the benighted prejudices of all nations and religions and must make known to every member of the human race that all are the leaves of one branch, the fruits of one bough.

Until such time, however, as the friends establish perfect unity among themselves, how can they summon others to harmony and peace?

Strive ye by day and night to cultivate your unity to the fullest degree. Let your thoughts dwell on your own spiritual development, and close your eyes to the deficiencies of other souls. Act ye in such wise, showing forth pure and goodly deeds, and modesty and humility, that ye will cause others to be awakened.

122   How good it is if the friends be as close as sheaves of light, if they stand together side by side in a firm unbroken line. For now have the rays of reality from the Sun of the world of existence, united in adoration all the worshippers of this light; and these rays have, through infinite grace, gathered all peoples together within this wide-spreading shelter; therefore must all souls become as one soul, and all hearts as one heart. Let all be set free from the multiple identities that were born of passion and desire, and in the oneness of their love for God find a new way of life.

123   Be in perfect unity. Never become angry with one another. Let your eyes be directed toward the kingdom of truth and not toward the world of creation. Love the creatures for the sake of God and not for themselves. You will never be angry or impatient if you love them for the sake of God. Humanity is not perfect. There are imperfections in every human being, and you will always become unhappy if you look toward the people themselves. But if you look toward God, you will love them and be kind to them, for the world of God is the world of perfection and complete mercy. Therefore, do not look at the shortcomings of anybody; see with the sight of forgiveness. The imperfect eye beholds imperfections. The eye that covers faults looks toward the Creator of souls. He created them, trains and provides for them, endows them with capacity and life, sight and hearing; therefore, they are the signs of His grandeur.

124 IT BEHOVETH YOU to seek agreement and to be united; it behoveth you to be in close communion one with the other, at one both in body and soul, till ye match the Pleiades or a string of lustrous pearls. Then will ye be solidly established; thus will your words prevail, your star shine out, and your hearts be comforted.

125 THE CONSCIOUSNESS of any division or cleavage in its [the Bahá'í community's] ranks is alien to its very purpose, principles, and ideals. Once its members have fully recognized the claim of its Author, and, by identifying themselves with its Administrative Order, accepted unreservedly the principles and laws embodied in its teachings, every differentiation of class, creed, or colour must automatically be obliterated, and never be allowed, under any pretext, and however great the pressure of events or of public opinion, to reassert itself.

126 THE CAUSE . . . is growing very rapidly, and the more it spreads the more the attention of the public will be fixed upon it. This imposes a heavy responsibility on the believers, as they must show forth such a spirit of love and unity among themselves as will attract the hearts of others and encourage them to enter the Faith in large numbers. We must always remember that the Teachings are perfect, and that the only reason more of our fellowmen have not as yet embraced them is because we Bahá'ís, the world over, are ourselves not yet as selfless and radiant mirrors of Bahá'u'lláh's Truth as we should and could be. We must constantly strive to better exemplify His Teachings.

127 INDEED THE BELIEVERS have not yet fully learned to draw on each other's love for strength and consolation in time of need. The Cause of God is endowed with tremendous powers, and the reason

Be in perfect unity. Never become angry with one another. Let your eyes be directed toward the kingdom of truth and not toward the world of creation. Love the creatures for the sake of God and not for themselves. You will never be angry or impatient if you love them for the sake of God. Humanity is not perfect.

the believers do not gain more from it is because they have not learned to draw fully on these mighty forces of love and strength and harmony generated by the Faith.

128 Bahá'u'lláh tells us that prejudice in its various forms destroys the edifice of humanity. We are adjured by the Divine Messenger to eliminate all forms of prejudice from our lives. Our outer lives must show forth our beliefs. The world must see that, regardless of each passing whim or current fashion of the generality of mankind, the Bahá'í lives his life according to the tenets of his Faith. We must not allow the fear of rejection by our friends and neighbours to deter us from our goal: to live the Bahá'í life. Let us strive to blot out from our lives every last trace of prejudice – racial, religious, political, economic, national, tribal, class, cultural, and that which is based on differences of education or age. We shall be distinguished from our non-Bahá'í associates if our lives are adorned with this principle.

If we allow prejudice of any kind to manifest itself in us, we shall be guilty before God of causing a setback to the progress and real growth of the Faith of Bahá'u'lláh. It is incumbent upon every believer to endeavour with a fierce determination to eliminate this defect from his thoughts and acts. It is the duty of the institutions of the Faith to inculcate this principle in the hearts of the friends through every means at their disposal including summer schools, conferences, institutes and study classes.

8

THE ROLE OF THE BAHÁ'Í COMMUNITY IN ESTABLISHING WORLD UNITY

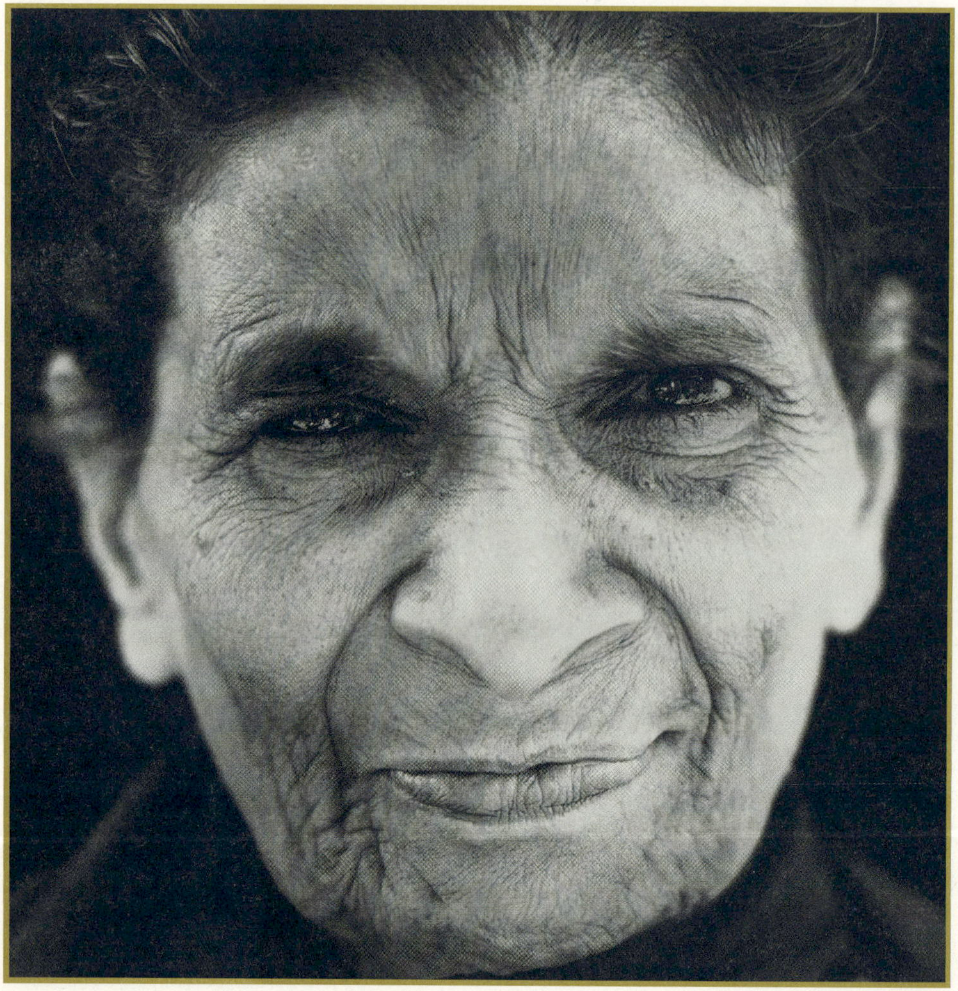

129 Consort with all men, O people of Bahá, in a spirit of friendliness and fellowship.

130 They that are endued with sincerity and faithfulness should associate with all the peoples and kindreds of the earth with joy and radiance, inasmuch as consorting with people hath promoted and will continue to promote unity and concord, which in turn are conducive to the maintenance of order in the world and to the regeneration of nations.

131 O people of Justice! Be as brilliant as the light and as splendid as the fire that blazed in the Burning Bush. The brightness of the fire of your love will no doubt fuse and unify the contending peoples and kindreds of the earth, whilst the fierceness of the flame of enmity and hatred cannot but result in strife and ruin.

132 He Who is the Eternal Truth hath, from the Dayspring of Glory, directeth His eyes towards the people of Bahá, and is addressing them in these words: 'Address yourselves to the promotion of the well-being and tranquillity of the children of men. Bend your minds and wills to the education of the peoples and kindreds of the earth, that haply the dissensions that divide it may, through the power of the Most Great Name, be blotted out from its face, and mankind become the upholders of one Order, and the inhabitants of one City. Illumine and hallow your hearts; let them not be profaned by the thorns of hate or the thistles of malice. Ye dwell in one world, and have been created through the operation of one Will. Blessed is he who mingleth with all men in a spirit of utmost kindliness and love.'

Bend your minds and wills to the education of the peoples and kindreds of the earth, that haply the dissensions that divide it may, through the power of the Most Great Name, be blotted out from its face, and mankind become the upholders of one Order, and the inhabitants of one City.

133 IF A SMALL NUMBER OF PEOPLE gather lovingly together, with absolute purity and sanctity, with their hearts free of the world, experiencing the emotions of the Kingdom and the powerful magnetic forces of the Divine, and being at one in their happy fellowship, that gathering will exert its influence over all the earth. The nature of that band of people, the words they speak, the deeds they do, will unleash the bestowals of Heaven, and provide a foretaste of eternal bliss. The hosts of the Company on high will defend them, and the angels of the Abhá Paradise, in continuous succession, will come down to their aid.

134 IN EVERY DISPENSATION, there hath been the commandment of fellowship and love, but it was a commandment limited to the community of those in mutual agreement, not to the dissident foe. In this wondrous age, however, praised be God, the commandments of God are not delimited, not restricted to any one group of people, rather have all the friends been commanded to show forth loving-kindness to every community on earth.

135 NOW MUST the lovers of God arise to carry out these instructions of His: let them be kindly fathers to the children of the human race, and compassionate brothers to the youth, and self-denying off-spring to those bent with years. The meaning of this is that ye must show forth tenderness and love to every human being, even to your enemies, and welcome them all with unalloyed friendship, good cheer, and loving-kindness.

136 O YE LOVED ONES of the Lord! This is the hour when ye must associate with all the earth's peoples in extreme kindliness and love, and be to them the signs and tokens of God's great mercy. Ye must become the very soul of the world, the living spirit in the body of the children of men.

137 O YE LOVERS of this wronged one! Cleanse ye your eyes, so that ye behold no man as different from yourselves. See ye no strangers; rather see all men as friends, for love and unity come hard when ye fix your gaze on otherness.

138 NOW IS THE TIME for the lovers of God to raise high the banners of unity, to intone, in the assemblages of the world, the verses of friendship and love and to demonstrate to all that the grace of God is one. Thus will the tabernacles of holiness be upraised on the summits of the earth, gathering all peoples into the protective shadow of the Word of Oneness.

139 CONSORT TOGETHER in brotherly love, be ready to lay down your lives one for the other, and not only for those who are dear to you, but for all humanity. Look upon the whole human race as members of one family, all children of God; and, in so doing, you will see no difference between them.

140 LOVE YE ALL religions and all races with a love that is true and sincere and show that love through deeds and not through the tongue; for the latter hath no importance, as the majority of men are, in speech, well-wishers, while action is best.

141 CONSORT WITH ALL THE PEOPLES, kindreds and religions of the world with the utmost truthfulness, uprightness, faithfulness, kindliness, good-will and friendliness, that all the world of being may be filled with the holy ecstasy of the grace of Bahá, that ignorance, enmity, hate and rancour may vanish from the world and the darkness of estrangement amidst the peoples and kindreds of the world may give way to the Light of Unity.

> *Cleanse ye your eyes, so that ye behold no man as different from yourselves. See ye no strangers; rather see all men as friends, for love and unity come hard when ye fix your gaze on otherness.*

142 STRIVE DAY AND NIGHT that animosity and contention may pass away from the hearts of men, that all religions shall become reconciled and the nations love each other so that no racial, religious or political prejudice may remain and the world of humanity behold God as the beginning and end of all existence. God has created all, and all return to God. Therefore, love humanity with all your heart and soul.

143 MAY WE UPHOLD THE FLAG of international agreement and enkindle a light which shall illumine all regions with the radiance of oneness. May our purposes centralize in the earnest desire of attaining the good pleasure of God, and may our supreme energies be directed to welding together the human household. Let us not regard our own respective capacities; nay rather, let us regard forever the favours and bounties of God.

144 OUR GREATEST EFFORTS must be directed towards detachment from the things of the world; we must strive to become more spiritual, more luminous, to follow the counsel of the Divine Teaching, to serve the cause of unity and true equality, to be merciful, to reflect the love of the Highest on all men, so that the light of the Spirit shall be apparent in all our deeds, to the end that all humanity shall be united, the stormy sea thereof calmed, and all rough waves disappear from off the surface of life's ocean henceforth unruffled and peaceful.

145 QUENCH YE the fires of war, lift high the banners of peace, work for the oneness of humankind and remember that religion is the channel of love unto all peoples. Be ye aware that the children of men are the sheep of God and He their loving Shepherd, that He careth tenderly for all His sheep and maketh

them to feed in His own green pastures of grace and giveth them to drink from the wellspring of life. Such is the way of the Lord. such are His bestowals. Such, from among His teachings, is His precept of the oneness of mankind.

146 UNLESS AND UNTIL the believers really come to realize they are one spiritual family, knit together by a bond more lasting than any more physical ties can ever be, they will not be able to create that warm community atmosphere which alone can attract the hearts of humanity, frozen for lack of real love and feeling.

147 MOST IMPORTANT OF ALL is that love and unity should prevail in the Bahá'í Community, as this is what people are most longing for in the present dark state of the world. Words without the living example will never be sufficient to breathe hope into the hearts of a disillusioned and often cynical generation.

148 THE GREAT THING is to 'live the life' – to have our lives so saturated with the Divine teachings and the Bahá'í spirit that people cannot fail to see a joy, a power, a love, a purity, a radiance, an efficiency in our character and work that will distinguish us from worldly-minded people and make people wonder what is the secret of this new life in us. We must become entirely selfless and devoted to God so that every day and every moment we seek to do only what God would have us do and the way He would have us do it. If we do this sincerely then we shall have perfect unity and harmony with each other. Where there is want of harmony, there is lack of the true Bahá'í Spirit. Unless we can show this transformation in our lives, this new power, this mutual love and harmony, then the Bahá'í teachings are but a name to us.

> *Quench ye the fires of war, lift high the banners of peace, work for the oneness of humankind and remember that religion is the channel of love unto all peoples.*

149   At one of the darkest periods in the prolonged oppression of the dearly-loved, resolutely steadfast friends in Iran, Shoghi Effendi was moved to comfort them in a letter of astounding insight. 'It is the shedding of the sacred blood of the martyrs in Persia' he wrote, 'which, in this shining era, this resplendent, this gem-studded Bahá'í age, shall change the face of the earth into high heaven and, as revealed in the Tablets, raise up the tabernacle of the oneness of mankind in the very heart of the world, reveal to men's eyes the reality of the unity of the human race . . .'

150   Two great processes are at work in the world: the great Plan of God, tumultuous in its progress, working through mankind as a whole, tearing down barriers to world unity and forging humankind into a unified body in the fires of suffering and experience. This process will produce, in God's due time, the Lesser Peace, the political unification of the world. Mankind at that time can be likened to a body that is unified but without life. The second process, the task of breathing life into this unified body – of creating true unity and spirituality culminating in the Most Great Peace – is that of the Bahá'ís, who are labouring consciously, with detailed instructions and continuing Divine guidance, to erect the fabric of the Kingdom of God on earth, into which they call their fellowmen, thus conferring upon them eternal life.

151   The experience of the Bahá'í community may be seen as an example of this enlarging unity. It is a community . . . drawn from many nations, cultures, classes and creeds, engaged in a wide range of activities serving the spiritual, social and economic needs of the peoples of many lands. It is a single social organism,

representative of the diversity of the human family, conducting its affairs through a system of commonly accepted consultative principles, and cherishing equally all the great outpourings of divine guidance in human history. Its existence is yet another convincing proof of the practicality of its Founder's vision of a united world, another evidence that humanity can live as one global society, equal to whatever challenges its coming of age may entail. If the Bahá'í experience can contribute in whatever measure to reinforcing hope in the unity of the human race, we are happy to offer it as a model for study.

> *If the Bahá'í experience can contribute in whatever measure to reinforcing hope in the unity of the human race, we are happy to offer it as a model for study.*

9

THE COVENANT;
AXIS OF THE ONENESS
OF HUMANITY

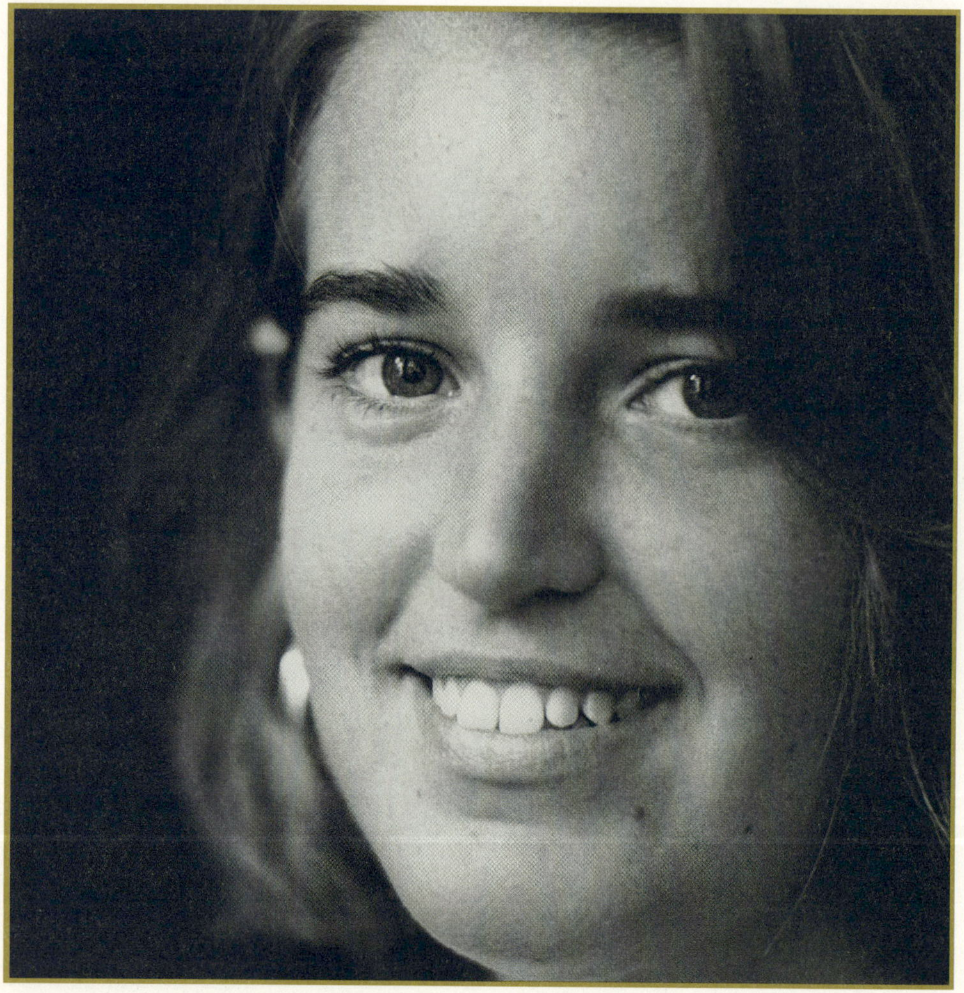

152   As to the most great characteristic of the revelation of Bahá'u'lláh, a specific teaching not given by any of the Prophets of the past: It is the ordination and appointment of the Centre of the Covenant. By this appointment and provision He has safeguarded and protected the religion of God against differences and schisms, making it impossible for anyone to create a new sect or faction of belief.

153   Today the dynamic power of the world of existence is the power of the Covenant which like unto an artery pulsateth in the body of the contingent world and protecteth Bahá'í unity.

154   Do not disrupt Bahá'í unity, and know that this unity cannot be maintained save through faith in the Covenant of God.

155   Today the most important principle of faith is firmness in the Covenant, because firmness in the Covenant wards off differences. Therefore, you must be firm as mountains.

156   It is indubitably clear . . . that the pivot of the oneness of mankind is nothing else but the power of the Covenant.

157   The power of the Covenant is as the heat of the sun which quickeneth and promoteth the development of all created things on earth. The light of the Covenant, in like manner, is the educator of the minds, the spirits, the hearts and the souls of men.

158   Today, the Lord of Hosts is the defender of the Covenant, the forces of the Kingdom protect it, heavenly souls tender their services, and heavenly angels promulgate and spread it broadcast. If it is considered with insight, it will be seen that all the forces of the universe, in the last analysis, serve the Covenant.

If it is considered with insight, it will be seen that all the forces of the universe, in the last analysis, serve the Covenant.

159 NO POWER can eliminate misunderstandings except that of the Covenant. The power of the Covenant is all-embracing, and resolveth all difficulties…

160 BAHÁ'U'LLÁH, the Revealer of God's Word in this Day, the Source of Authority, the Fountainhead of Justice, the Creator of a new World Order, the Establisher of the Most Great Peace, the Inspirer and Founder of a world civilization, the Judge, the Lawgiver, the Unifier and Redeemer of all mankind, has proclaimed the advent of God's Kingdom on earth, has formulated its laws and ordinances, enunciated its principles, and ordained its institutions. To direct and canalize the forces released by His Revelation He instituted His Covenant, whose power has preserved the integrity of His Faith, maintained its unity and stimulated its world-wide expansion…

161 ♦ ♦ ♦ THE CAUSE OF BAHÁ'U'LLÁH has been protected against the baneful effects of the misuse of the process of criticism; this has been done by the institution of the Covenant and by the provision of a universal administrative system which incorporates within itself the mechanisms for drawing out the constructive ideas of individuals and using them for the benefit of the entire system. Admonishing the people to uphold the unifying purpose of the Cause, Bahá'u'lláh, in the Book of His Covenant, addresses these poignant words to them: 'Let not the means of order be made the cause of confusion and the instrument of union an occasion for discord.' Such assertions emphasize a crucial point; it is this: In terms of the Covenant, dissidence is a moral and intellectual contradiction of the main objective animating the Bahá'í community, the establishment of the unity of humankind.

162   SUBLIME EMOTIONS surge in our hearts as we survey the dramatic history and amazing progress of these one hundred years. At the time of the passing of Bahá'u'lláh, the Bahá'í community was contained within the borders of no more than fifteen countries, the vast majority of its members living in His native Iran. The community now embraces the entire planet. We rejoice at the spirit of unity which is evident in its steady consolidation through the workings of the Administrative Order to which the Covenant has given birth. Our cumulated experience has clearly demonstrated the efficacy of the Covenant. The genuine unity it induces greatly encourages our expectation that all of humanity can and will be united.

163   THE FOUNDATION of our belief rests on our recognition of the sovereignty of God, the Unknowable Essence, the Supreme Creator, and on our submission to His will as revealed for this age by Bahá'u'lláh. To accept the Messenger of God in His Day and to abide by His bidding are the two essential, inseparable duties which each soul was created to fulfil. One exercises these twin duties by one's own choice, and by so doing performs an act which may be regarded as the highest expression of free will with which every human being is endowed by an all-loving Creator. The vehicle in this resplendent age for the practical fulfilment of these duties is the Covenant of Bahá'u'lláh. It is the instrument by which belief in Him is translated into constructive deeds. The oneness of humankind is the pivotal principle and ultimate goal of His mission. This principle means far more than the reawakening of the spirit of brotherhood and goodwill among people: 'It implies an organic change in the structure of present-day society, a change such as the world has not yet experienced.' The Covenant of Bahá'u'lláh embodies the spirit, instrumentality and method to

> *At the time of the passing of Bahá'u'lláh, the Bahá'í community was contained within the borders of no more than fifteen countries, the vast majority of its members living in His native Iran. The community now embraces the entire planet. We rejoice at the spirit of unity which is evident in its steady consolidation through the workings of the Administrative Order to which the Covenant has given birth.*

attain this essential goal…

    This Covenant is the guarantee against schism; that is why those who occasionally attempt to create a cleavage in the community utterly fail in the long run. Similarly, the incessant persecution the community has been forced to endure for more than a century in the land of Bahá'u'lláh's birth has not succeeded in destroying its identity or undermining its organic unity. The glorious, ultimate effect of this arrangement will be to ensure the establishment of the Kingdom of God on earth, as promised in the Holy Books of old and proclaimed by Bahá'u'lláh Himself.

164 THE COVENANT is the 'axis of the oneness of the world of humanity' because it preserves the unity and integrity of the Faith itself and protects it from being disrupted by individuals who are convinced that only their understanding of the Teachings is the right one – a fate that has overcome all past Revelations.

10

FOUNDATIONS OF UNITY

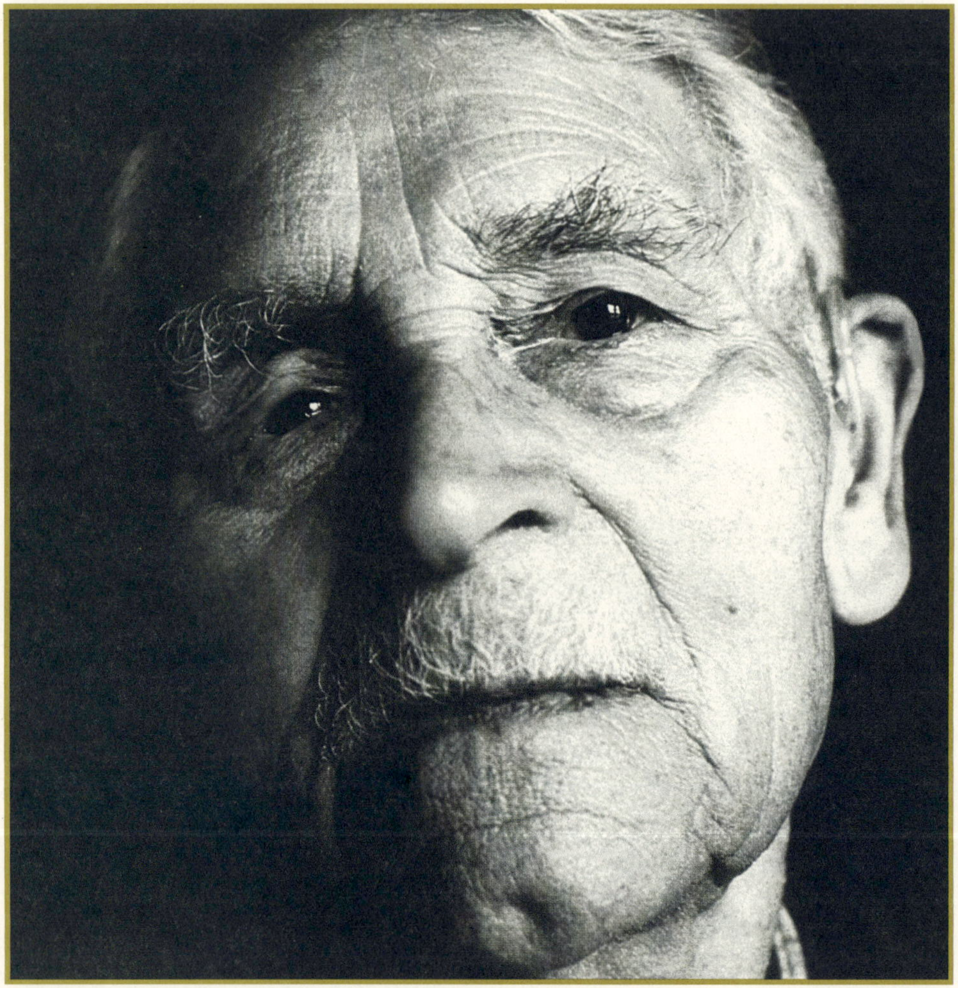

Marriage

165 THE LORD, peerless is He, hath made woman and man to abide with each other in the closest companionship, and to be even as a single soul. They are two helpmates, two intimate friends, who should be concerned about the welfare of each other.

166 THE FRIENDS OF GOD must so live and conduct themselves, and evince such excellence of character and conduct, as to make others astonished. The love between husband and wife must not be purely physical, nay, rather, it must be spiritual and heavenly. These two souls should be considered as one soul. How difficult it would be to divide a single soul! Nay, great would be the difficulty. In short, the foundation of the Kingdom of God is based upon harmony and love, oneness, relationship and union, not upon differences, especially between husband and wife. If one of these two becomes the cause of divorce, that one will unquestionably fall into great difficulties, will become the victim of formidable calamities and experience deep remorse.

167 BAHÁ'U'LLÁH has urged marriage upon all people as the natural and rightful way of life. He has also, however, placed strong emphasis on its spiritual nature, which, while in no way precluding a normal physical life, is the most essential aspect of marriage. That two people should live their lives in love and harmony is of far greater importance than that they should be consumed with passion for each other. The one is a great rock of strength on which to lean in time of need; the other a purely temporary thing which may at any time die out.

In short, the foundation of the Kingdom of God is based upon harmony and love, oneness, relationship and union, not upon differences, especially between husband and wife.

168   Bahá'u'lláh has clearly stated the consent of all living parents is required for a Bahá'í marriage. This applies whether the parents are Bahá'ís or non-Bahá'ís, divorced for years or not. This great law He has laid down to strengthen the social fabric, to knit closer the ties of the home, to place a certain gratitude and respect in the hearts of children for those who have given them life and sent their should out on the eternal journey towards their Creator. We Bahá'ís must realize that in present-day society the exact opposite process is taking place: young people care less and less for their parents' wishes, divorce is considered a natural right, and obtained on the flimsiest and most unwarrantable and shabby pretexts. People separated from each other, especially if one of them has had full custody of the children, are only too willing to belittle the importance of the partner in marriage also responsible as a parent for bringing those children into this world. The Bahá'ís must, through rigid adherence to the Bahá'í laws and teachings, combat these corrosive forces which are so rapidly destroying home life and the beauty of family relationships, and tearing down the moral structure of society.

169   Marriage is a very sacred institution. Bahá'u'lláh said its purpose is to promote unity.

The Family

170   Note ye how easily, where unity existeth in a given family, the affairs of that family are conducted; what progress the members of that family make, how they prosper in the world. Their concerns are in order, they enjoy comfort and tranquillity, they are secure, their position is assured, they come to be envied

by all. Such a family but addeth to its stature and its lasting honour, as day succeedeth day.

171 IF LOVE AND AGREEMENT are manifest in a single family, that family will advance, become illumined and spiritual; but if enmity and hatred exist within it destruction and dispersion are inevitable.

172 REGARDING the Bahá'í teachings on divorce. While the latter has been made permissible by Bahá'u'lláh yet He has strongly discouraged its practice, for if not checked and seriously controlled it leads gradually to the disruption of family life and to the disintegration of society.

173 IT IS ONE OF THE ESSENTIAL TEACHINGS of the Faith that unity should be maintained in the home. Of course this does not mean that any member of the family has a right to influence that faith of any other member; and if this is realized by all the members, then it seems certain that unity would be feasible.

174 WHEREVER THERE IS a Bahá'í family, those concerned should by all means do all they can to preserve it. Because divorce is strongly condemned in the Teachings, whereas harmony, unity and love are held up as the highest ideals in human relationships.

175 BAHÁ'U'LLÁH came to bring unity to the world, and a fundamental unity is that of the family. Therefore, one must believe that the Faith is intended to strengthen the family, not weaken it, and one of the keys to the strengthening of unity is loving consultation. The atmosphere within a Bahá'í family as within the community as a whole should express 'the keynote of

---

Bahá'u'lláh came to bring unity to the world, and a fundamental unity is that of the family. Therefore, one must believe that the Faith is intended to strengthen the family, not weaken it, and one of the keys to the strengthening of unity is loving consultation.

the Cause of God' which, the beloved Guardian has stated, 'is not dictatorial authority but humble fellowship, not arbitrary power, but the spirit of frank and loving consultation.

The Nineteen Day Feast

176 Verily, it is enjoined upon you to offer a feast, once in every month, though only water be served; for God hath purposed to bind hearts together, albeit through both earthly and heavenly means.

177 As to the Nineteen Day Feast, ye must give this your most careful attention, and firmly establish it. For this Feast bringeth bliss and unity and love to the lovers of God.

178 This Feast is a bringer of joy. It is the groundwork of agreement and unity. It is the key to affection and fellowship. It diffuseth the oneness of mankind.

179 You have asked as to the feast in every Bahá'í month. This feast is held to foster comradeship and love, to call God to mind and supplicate Him with contrite hearts, and to encourage benevolent pursuits. That is, the friends should there dwell upon God and glorify Him, read the prayers and holy verses, and treat one another with the utmost affection and love. Should trouble arise between two of the friends, let both be invited in, and efforts made to compose their differences. Let all discussion centre on the doing of charitable acts and holy deeds, that laudable results may be the fruit thereof.

180 You must continue to keep the Nineteen Day Feast. It is very important; it is very good. But when you present yourselves in the meetings, before entering them, free yourselves from all that you have in your heart, free your thoughts and your minds from all else save God, and speak to your heart. That all may make this a gathering of love, make it the cause of illumination, make it a gathering of attraction of the hearts, surround this gathering with the Lights of the Supreme Concourse, so that you may be gathered together with the utmost love.

181 Each one of you must think how to make happy and pleased the other members of your Assembly, and each one must consider all those who are present as better and greater than himself, and each one must consider himself less than the rest. Know their station as high, and think of your own station as low. Should you act and live according to these behests, know verily, of a certainty, that that Feast is the Heavenly Food. That Supper is the 'Lord's Supper!' I am the Servant of that gathering.

182 The Nineteen Day Feast was inaugurated by the Báb and ratified by Bahá'u'lláh, in His holy book, the Aqdas, so that people may gather together and outwardly show fellowship and love, that the divine mysteries may be disclosed. The object is concord, that through this fellowship hearts may become perfectly united, and reciprocity and mutual helpfulness be established. Because the members of the world of humanity are unable to exist without being banded together, cooperation and mutual helpfulness is the basis of human society. Without the realization of these two great principles no great movement is pressed forward…

This Feast is a bringer of joy. It is the groundwork of agreement and unity. It is the key to affection and fellowship. It diffuseth the oneness of mankind.

183   IN BRIEF, this is my hope: that the Nineteen Day Feast become the cause of great spiritual solidarity between the friends, that it may bring believers into the bond of unity, and we will then be so united together that love and wisdom will spread from this centre to all parts. This Feast is a divine Feast. It is a Lord's supper. It attracts confirmation of God like a magnet. It is the cause of the enlightenment of hearts.

184   EVERY MEETING which is organized for the purpose of unity and concord will be conducive to changing strangers into friends, enemies into associates, and 'Abdu'l-Bahá will be present in His heart and soul at that meeting.

185   THE WORLD ORDER of Bahá'u'lláh encompasses all units of human society; integrates the spiritual, administrative and social processes of life; and canalizes human expression in its varied forms towards the construction of a new civilization. The Nineteen Day Feast embraces all these aspects at the very base of society. Functioning in the village, the town, the city, it is an institution of which all the people of Bahá are members. It is intended to promote unity, ensure progress, and foster joy.

186   IT IS CLEAR, THEN, that the Feast is rooted in hospitality, with all its implications of friendliness, courtesy, service, generosity and conviviality. The very idea of hospitality as the sustaining spirit of so significant an institution introduces a revolutionary new attitude to the conduct of human affairs at all levels, an attitude which is so critical to that world unity which the Central Figures of our Faith laboured so long and suffered so much cruelty to bring into being. It is in this divine festival that the foundation is laid for the realization of so unprecedented a reality. That you may all

attain the high mark set for the Feast as a 'bringer of joy', the 'groundwork of agreement and unity', the 'key to affection and fellowship' will remain an object of our ardent supplications at the Holy Threshold.

Spiritual Assemblies

187 THE FIRST DUTY of the members is to effect their own unity and harmony, in order to obtain good results. If there be no unity, or the Committee becomes the cause of inharmony, undoubtedly, it is better that it does not exist….

Therefore, when the unity of the members … is established, their second duty is to read the verses and communes, to be in a state of commemoration and mindfulness, that they may see each other as if in the presence of God.

188 THE HONOURED MEMBERS of the Spiritual Assembly should exert their efforts so that no differences may occur, and if such differences do occur, they should not reach the point of causing conflict, hatred and antagonism, which lead to threats. When you notice that a stage has been reached when enmity and threats are about to occur, you should immediately postpone discussion of the subject, until wranglings, disputations, and loud talk vanish, and a propitious time is at hand.

189 THE PRIME REQUISITES for them that take counsel together are purity of motive, radiance of spirit, detachment from all else save God, attraction to His Divine Fragrances, humility and lowliness amongst His loved ones, patience and long-suffering in difficulties and servitude to His exalted Threshold. Should they be

---

The World Order of Bahá'u'lláh encompasses all units of human society; integrates the spiritual, administrative and social processes of life; and canalizes human expression in its varied forms towards the construction of a new civilization. The Nineteen Day Feast embraces all these aspects at the very base of society.

graciously aided to acquire these attributes, victory from the unseen Kingdom of Bahá shall be vouchsafed to them ... The members thereof must take counsel together in such wise that no occasion for ill-feeling or discord may arise. This can be attained when every member expresseth with absolute freedom his own opinion and setteth forth his argument. Should any one oppose, he must on no account feel hurt for not until matters are fully discussed can the right way be revealed. The shining spark of truth cometh forth only after the clash of differing opinions. If after discussion, a decision be carried unanimously, well and good; but if, the Lord forbid, differences of opinion should arise, a majority of voices must prevail.

190 ♦ ♦ ♦ CONSULTATION MUST HAVE for its object the investigation of truth. He who expresses an opinion should not voice it as correct and right but set it forth as a contribution to the consensus of opinion; for the light of reality becomes apparent when two opinions coincide. A spark is produced when flint and steel come together. Man should weigh his opinions with the utmost serenity, calmness and composure. Before expressing his own views he should carefully consider the views already advanced by others. If he finds that a previously expressed opinion is more true and worthy, he should accept it immediately and not wilfully hold to an opinion of his own. By this excellent method he endeavours to arrive at unity and truth. ... Therefore, true consultation is spiritual conference in the attitude and atmosphere of love. Members must love each other in the spirit of fellowship in order that good results may be forthcoming. Love and fellowship are the foundation.

191   THEY MUST WHEN COMING TOGETHER turn their faces to the Kingdom on High and ask aid from the Realm of Glory. They must then proceed with the utmost devotion, courtesy, dignity, care and moderation to express their views. They must in every matter search out the truth and not insist upon their own opinion, for stubbornness and persistence in one's views will lead ultimately to discord and wrangling and the truth will remain hidden. The honoured members must with all freedom express their own thoughts, and it is in no wise permissible for one to belittle the thought of another, nay, he must with moderation set forth the truth, and should differences of opinion arise a majority of voices must prevail, and all must obey and submit to the majority. It is again not permitted that any one of the honoured members object to or censure, whether in or out of the meeting, any decision arrived at previously, though that decision be not right, for such criticism would prevent any decision from being enforced. In short, whatsoever thing is arranged in harmony and with love and purity of motive, its result is light, and should the least trace of estrangement prevail the result shall be darkness upon darkness... If this be so regarded, that assembly shall be of God, but otherwise it shall lead to coolness and alienation that proceed from the Evil One... Should they endeavour to fulfil these conditions the Grace of the Holy Spirit shall be vouchsafed unto them, and that assembly shall become the centre of the Divine blessings, the hosts of Divine confirmation shall come to their aid, and they shall day by day receive a new effusion of Spirit.

192   INDEED, IT HAS EVER BEEN the cherished desire of our Master, 'Abdu'l-Bahá, that the friends in their councils, local as well as national, should by their candour, their honesty of purpose, their singleness of mind, and the thoroughness of their discussions, achieve unanimity in all things.

> *The shining spark of truth cometh forth only after the clash of differing opinions. If after discussion, a decision be carried unanimously, well and good; but if, the Lord forbid, differences of opinion should arise, a majority of voices must prevail.*

193 ONCE THE ASSEMBLY, through a majority vote of its members, comes to a decision the friends should readily obey it. Specially those dissenting members within the Assembly whose opinion is contrary to that of the majority of their fellow-members should set a good example before the community by sacrificing their personal views for the sake of obeying the principle of majority vote that underlies the functioning of all Bahá'í Assemblies.

But before the majority of the Assembly comes to a decision, it is not only the right but the sacred obligation of every member to express freely and openly his views, without being afraid of displeasing or alienating any of his fellow-members.

194 THROUGH THE CLASH of personal opinions, as 'Abdu'l-Bahá has stated, the spark of truth is often ignited, and Divine guidance revealed. The friends should therefore not feel discouraged at the differences of opinion that may prevail among the members of an Assembly, for these, as experience has shown, and as the Master's words attest, fulfil a valuable function in all Assembly deliberations. But once the opinion of the majority has been ascertained, all the members should automatically and unreservedly obey it, and faithfully carry it out. Patience and restraint, however, should at all times characterize the discussions and deliberations of the elected representatives of the local community, and no fruitless and hair-splitting discussions indulged in, under any circumstances.

195 WE ALL HAVE A RIGHT to our opinions, we are bound to think differently; but a Bahá'í must accept the majority decision of his Assembly, realizing that acceptance and harmony – even if a mistake has been made – are the really important things, and

when we serve the Cause properly, in the Bahá'í way, God will right any wrongs done in the end.

…Bahá'ís are not required to vote on an Assembly against their consciences. It is better if they submit to the majority view and make it unanimous. But they are not forced to. What they must do, however, is to abide by the majority decision, as this is what becomes effective. They must not go around undermining the Assembly by saying they disagreed with the majority. In other words, they must put the Cause first and not their own opinions. He (a Spiritual Assembly member) can ask the Assembly to reconsider a matter, but he has no right to force them or create inharmony because they won't change. Unanimous votes are preferable, but certainly cannot be forced upon Assembly members by artificial methods such as are used by other societies.

196 IT IS IMPORTANT to realise that the spirit of Bahá'í consultation is very different from that current in the decision-making processes of non-Bahá'í bodies.

The ideal of Bahá'í consultation is to arrive at a unanimous decision. When this is not possible a vote must be taken. In the words of the beloved Guardian:

> …when they are called upon to arrive at a certain decision, they should, after dispassionate, anxious and cordial consultation, turn to God in prayer, and with earnestness and conviction and courage record their vote and abide by the voice of the majority, which we are told by the Master to be the voice of truth, never to be challenged, and always to be whole-heartedly enforced. As soon as a decision is reached it becomes the decision of the whole Assembly, not merely of those members who happened to be among the majority.

We all have a right to our opinions, we are bound to think differently; but a Bahá'í must accept the majority decision of his Assembly, realizing that acceptance and harmony – even if a mistake has been made – are the really important things, and when we serve the Cause properly, in the Bahá'í way, God will right any wrongs done in the end.

197 THE UNITY we are called upon to achieve in Bahá'í service is a harmony which is produced through active participation in the work of the Cause, not through withdrawal from activity, or resignation from Assemblies and Committees. By looking for the good in others, by praising and encouraging our fellow believers in their endeavours, by acting mercifully and lovingly towards them, forgiving instead of insisting that they be brought to justice because we feel they may have wronged us, by trying all the time to purify the motives of our conduct in the hope that our services will be acceptable in the sight of Bahá'u'lláh, and by constant prayer that He may forgive our shortcomings and aid us to radiantly, patiently and selflessly promote the vital interests of our Cause, we can become sources of unity in the community and instruments in the hands of the Almighty to use according to His Will and Purpose.

198 ONE OF THE QUESTIONS that should remain uppermost in the minds of the Assembly, the committees and the individual friends is how to uphold at all times, through their functions and deeds, the primary principle and goal of our Faith, namely, the unity of the human race.

11

Individual Responsibility for Maintaining Unity Among Bahá'ís

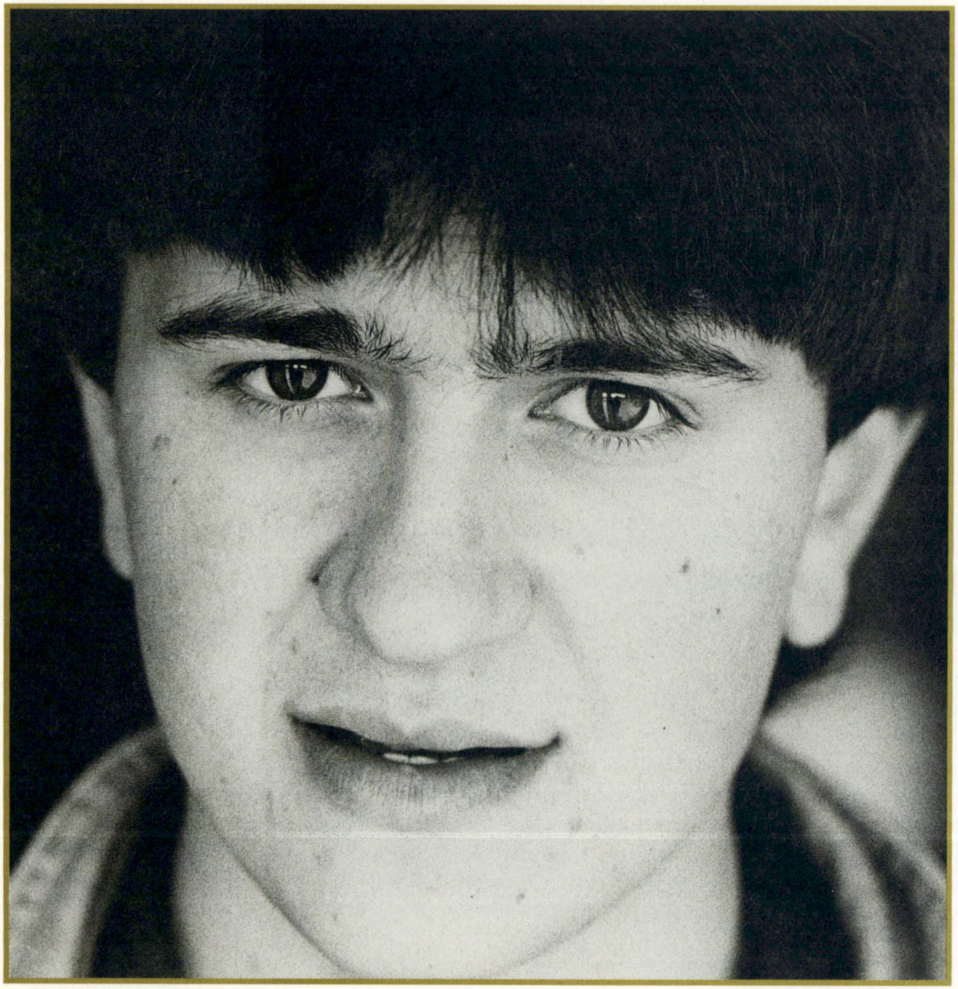

199 BEWARE LEST THE DESIRES of the flesh and of a corrupt inclination provoke divisions among you. Be ye as the fingers of one hand, the members of one body.

200 EVERY EYE, in this Day, should seek what will best promote the Cause of God. He, Who is the Eternal Truth, beareth Me witness! Nothing whatever can, in this Day, inflict a greater harm upon this Cause than dissension and strife, contention, estrangement and apathy, among the loved ones of God. Flee them, through the power of God and His Sovereign aid, and strive ye to knit together the hearts of men, in His Name, the Unifier, the All-Knowing, the All-Wise.

201 IF TWO SOULS QUARREL and contend about a question of the Divine questions, differing and disputing, both are wrong. The wisdom of this incontrovertible law of God is this: That between two souls from amongst the believers of God, no contention and dispute may arise; that they may speak with each other with infinite amity and love.

202 THE OFT-REPEATED WORDS of the Master concerning unity and harmonious cooperation among the friends should be carefully and thoughtfully remembered now more than ever. Nothing is more contrary to the spirit of the Cause than discord and strife, which are the inevitable outcome of selfishness and greed. Pure detachment and selfless service, these should be the sole motives of every true believer. And unless each and every one of the friends succeeds in translating such qualities into living action, no hope of further progress can be entertained. It is now that unity of thought and action is most needed.

If two souls quarrel and contend about a question of the Divine questions, differing and disputing, both are wrong.

203 SURELY, THE BELIEVERS, no matter how qualified they may be, whether as teachers or administrators, and however high their intellectual and spiritual merits, should never be looked upon as a standard whereby to evaluate and measure the divine authority and mission of the Faith. It is to the Teachings themselves, and to the lives of the Founders of the Cause that the believers should look for their guidance and inspiration, and only by keeping strictly to such true attitude can they hope to establish their loyalty to Bahá'u'lláh upon an enduring and unassailable basis. You should take heart, therefore, and with unrelaxing vigilance and unremitting effort endeavour to play your full share in the gradual unfoldment of this Divine World Order.

204 THE FRIENDS MUST BE PATIENT with each other and must realize that the Cause is still in its infancy and its institutions are not yet functioning perfectly. The greater the patience, the loving understanding and the forbearance the believers show towards each other and their shortcomings, the greater will be the progress of the whole Bahá'í Community at large.

205 IN THE LIFE OF ANY COMMUNITY, especially an immature Community such as that of the Bahá'ís at present – still in its infancy, so to speak – there are bound to be all kinds of things arise which are disturbing to some of the friends and a test to them. The main thing is that they should never allow such things to disturb that fundamental sense of unity and spiritual kinship which should underlie all Bahá'í Community life. We must realize our imperfection and not permit ourselves to get too upset over the unfortunate things which occur, sometimes in Conventions, sometimes in Assemblies or on Committees, etc. Such things are essentially superficial and in time will be outgrown.

206 THE GUARDIAN BELIEVES that a great deal of the difficulties from which the believers . . . feel themselves to be suffering are caused by their neither correctly understanding nor putting into practice the administration. They seem – many of them – to be prone to continually challenging and criticizing the decisions of their Assemblies. If the Bahá'ís undermine the very leaders which are, however immaturely, seeking to coordinate Bahá'í activities and administer Bahá'í affairs, if they continually criticize their acts and challenge or belittle their decisions, they not only prevent any real rapid progress in the Faith's development from taking place, but they repel outsiders who quite rightly may ask how we ever expect to unite the whole world when we are so disunited among ourselves!

There is only one remedy for this: to study the administration, to obey the Assemblies, and each believer seek to perfect his own character as a Bahá'í. We can never exert the influence over others which we can exert over ourselves. If we are better, if we show love, patience, and understanding of the weaknesses of others; if we seek to never criticize but rather encourage, others will do likewise, and we can really help the Cause through our example and spiritual strength. The Bahá'ís everywhere, when the administration is first established, find it very difficult to adjust themselves. They have to learn to obey, even when the Assembly may be wrong, for the sake of unity. They have to sacrifice their personalities, to a certain extent, in order that the community life may grow and develop as a whole. These things are difficult – but we must realize that they will lead us to a very much greater; more perfect, way of life when the Faith is properly established according to the administration.

> *It is to the Teachings themselves, and to the lives of the Founders of the Cause that the believers should look for their guidance and inspiration, and only by keeping strictly to such true attitude can they hope to establish their loyalty to Bahá'u'lláh upon an enduring and unassailable basis.*

207 ONE OF THE MOST PARAMOUNT needs of the Cause ... is that the friends should unite, should become really keenly conscious of the fact that they are one spiritual family, held together by bonds more sacred and eternal than those physical ties which make people of the same family. If the friends will forget all personal differences and open their hearts to a great love for each other for the sake of Bahá'u'lláh, they will find that their powers are vastly increased, they will attract the heart of the public, and will witness a rapid growth of the Holy Faith ...

208 REGARDING YOUR QUESTION about the need for greater unity among the friends, there is no doubt that this is so, and the Guardian feels that one of the chief instruments for promoting it is to teach the Bahá'ís themselves, in classes and through precepts, that love of God, and consequently of men, is the essential foundation of every religion, our own included. A greater degree of love will produce a greater unity, because it enables people to bear with each other, to be patient and forgiving.

209 SO MANY MISUNDERSTANDINGS arise from the passionate attachment of the friends to the Faith and also their immaturity. We must therefore be very patient and loving with each other and try to establish unity in the Bahá'í family...

    He urges you to do your utmost to create a greater love and harmony in the Community, and to persevere in teaching the Holy Faith.

210 REGARDING the ... inharmony that seems to exist among certain of the friends ... when Bahá'ís permit the dark forces of the world to enter into their own relationships within the Faith they gravely jeopardize its progress; it is the paramount duty of the

believers, the local assemblies, and particularly the National Spiritual Assembly to foster harmony, understanding and love amongst the friends. All should be ready and willing to set aside every personal sense of grievance – justified or unjustified – for the good of the Cause, because the people will never embrace it until they see in its community life mirrored what is so conspicuously lacking in the world: love and unity.

211 THE BELIEVERS, to better understand their own internal condition, should realize that the forces of darkness in the world are so prevalent and strong that their morbid and turbulent influence is felt by all. They should therefore consciously strive to be more loving, more united, more dedicated and prayerful than ever before in order to fight against the atmosphere of present day society which is unloving, disunited, careless of right and wrong, and heedless of God.

212 THE THING THE FRIENDS NEED – everywhere – is a greater love for each other, and this can be acquired by greater love for Bahá'u'lláh; for if we love Him deeply enough, we will never allow personal feelings and opinions to hold His Cause back; we will be willing to sacrifice ourselves to each other for the sake of the Faith, and be as the Master said, one soul in many bodies.

213 WE MUST NEVER DWELL TOO MUCH on the attitudes and feelings of our fellow-believers towards us. What is most important is to foster love and harmony and ignore any rebuffs we may receive; in this way the weaknesses of human nature and the peculiarity or attitude of any particular person is not magnified, but pales into insignificance in comparison with our joint service to the Faith we all love.

> *A greater degree of love will produce a greater unity, because it enables people to bear with each other, to be patient and forgiving.*

214   Y̲ou must not make the great mistake of judging our Faith by one community which obviously needs to study and obey the Bahá'í teachings. Human frailties and peculiarities can be a great test. But the only way or perhaps I should say the first and best way, to remedy such situations is to oneself do what is right. One soul can be the cause of the spiritual illumination of a continent. Now that you have seen, and remedied a great fault in your own life, now that you see more clearly what is lacking in your own community, there is nothing to prevent you from arising and showing such an example, such a love and spirit of service, as to enkindle the hearts of your fellow Bahá'ís. He urges you to study deeply the teachings, teach others, study with those Bahá'ís who are anxious to do so the deeper teachings of our Faith, and through example, effort and prayer bring about a change.

215   T̲he best remedy for hate is love, as hate is the absence of love! In this respect you must show forth the love of God to others, Bahá'ís and non-Bahá'ís alike, and thus do your part to dispel the darkness in this world. This is what the beloved Master expects of His servants.

216   H̲owever, he feels very strongly that if …is in the state your letter would seem to indicate, it is certainly conducting its affairs in the wrong way. This does not mean the assembly, it means everyone. For where is Bahá'í love? Where is putting unity and harmony first? Where is willingness to sacrifice one's personal feelings and opinions to achieve love and harmony? What makes the Bahá'ís think that when they sacrifice the spiritual laws the administrative laws are going to work?

    He urges you to exert your utmost to get the … Bahá'ís to put aside such obnoxious terms as 'radical', 'conservative', 'progressive', 'enemies of the Cause', 'squelching the teachings', etc. If they paused for one moment to think for what purpose the Báb and the martyrs gave their lives, and Bahá'u'lláh and the Master accepted so much suffering, they would never let such definitions and accusations cross their lips when speaking of each other. As long as the friends quarrel amongst themselves their efforts will not be blessed for they are disobeying God.

217 ♦ ♦ ♦ WE MUST REACH a spiritual plane where God comes first and great human passions are unable to turn us away from Him. All the time we see people who either through the force of hate or the passionate attachment they have to another person, sacrifice principle or bar themselves from the Path of God…

218 WE MUST LOVE GOD, and in this state, a general love for all men becomes possible. We cannot love each human being for himself, but our feeling towards humanity should be motivated by our love for the Father who created all men.

219 HE URGES YOU to do all you can to promote unity and love amongst the members of the Community there, as this seems to be their greatest need.

So often young communities, in their desire to administer the Cause, lose sight of the fact that these spiritual relationships are far more important and fundamental than the rules and regulations which must govern the conduct of the community affairs. The greatest need it seems everywhere inside the Cause is to impress upon the friends the need for love among them. There is a tendency to mix up the functions of the Administration and try to apply it in individual relationships, which is abortive, because the Assembly is a nascent House of Justice and is supposed

> *We must love God, and in this state, a general love for all men becomes possible. We cannot love each human being for himself, but our feeling towards humanity should be motivated by our love for the Father who created all men.*

to administer, according to the Teachings, the affairs of the community. But individuals toward each other are governed by love, unity, forgiveness and a sin-covering eye.

220 PERHAPS THE GREATEST TEST Bahá'ís are ever subjected to is from each other; but for the sake of the Master they should be ever ready to overlook each other's mistakes; apologize for harsh words they have uttered, forgive and forget. He strongly recommends to you this course of action.

221 IT IS THE STRONG FEELING of the House of Justice that as pioneers . . . you have an inescapable responsibility before God to search your souls in order to identify the cause or causes of the differences, and then to arise with purity of motive, and with courage and perseverance to change hatred and separation into love and unity, division and discord into fellowship and harmony. This can easily be done if each one of you determines to subordinate personal interests and feelings to the overall needs of the Cause of God and its welfare, and to make the necessary effort to forget and forgive the past…

As each of you strives sincerely to uphold these noble principles in his life, he should endeavour to encourage others, unobtrusively, through words and deeds, tempered by wisdom, and characterized by humility and love, so that the rest of the friends will soon realize the gracious benefits of obedience to God's commands, and the grave dangers of stubbornly refusing to merge one's will in God's Will, and of placing one's ego above what is His first choice for us.

It would be useful in your meditations on this subject to bear in mind that Bahá'u'lláh abhorred what He describes in the Kitáb-i-Íqán as the 'fire of hatred', and that He, the Manifestation of God, decided to retire to Sulaymáníyyih in order to 'avoid becoming a subject of discord among the faithful, a source of disturbance unto Our companions, the means of injury to any soul, or the cause of sorrow to any heart.' This is a clear indication of the vital importance He attached to the spirit of unity and harmony which He wished to instil in the innermost being of the friends.

. . . you have an inescapable responsibility before God to search your souls in order to identify the cause or causes of the differences, and then to arise with purity of motive, and with courage and perseverance to change hatred and separation into love and unity, division and discord into fellowship and harmony.

12

Avoiding Backbiting, Fault-finding and Criticism

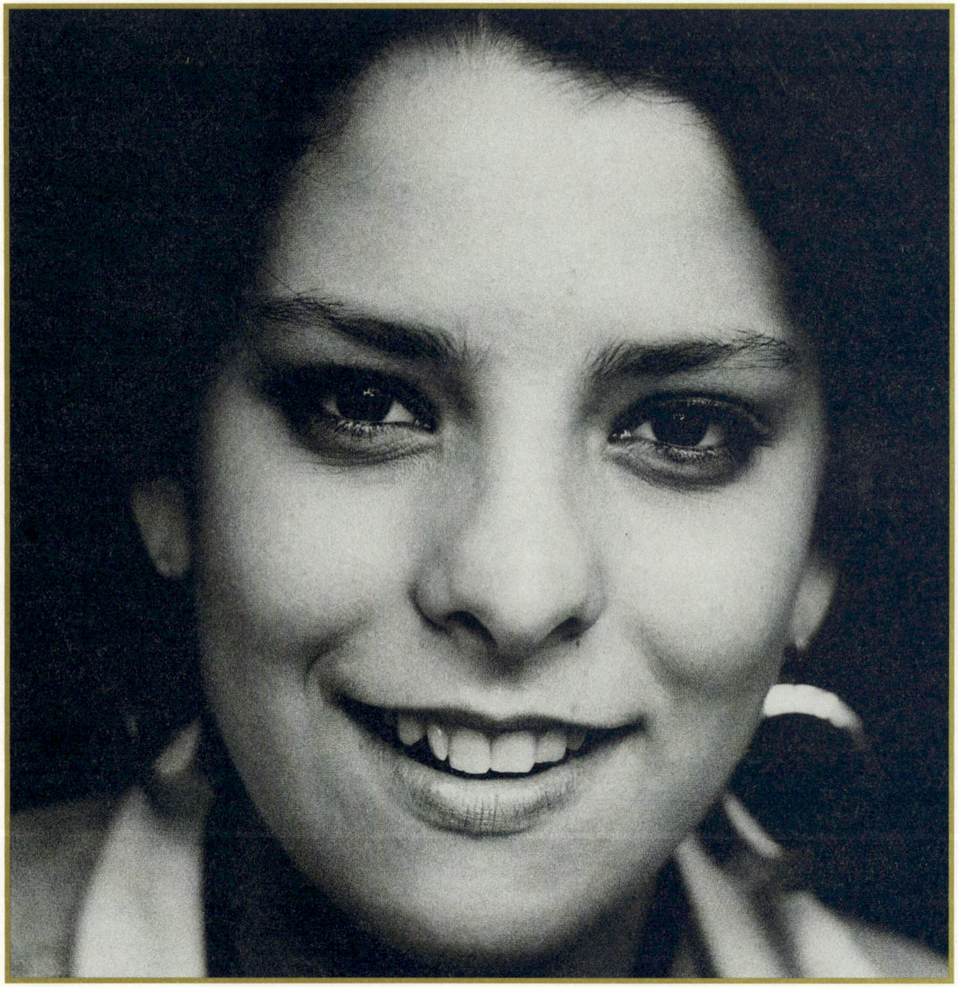

222   T͟HAT SEEKER must at all times put his trust in God … and refrain from idle talk. For the tongue is a smouldering fire, and excess of speech a deadly poison. Material fire consumeth the body, whereas the fire of the tongue devoureth both heart and soul. The force of the former lasteth but for a time, whilst the effects of the latter endure a century. That seeker should also regard backbiting as grievous error, and keep himself aloof from its dominion, inasmuch as backbiting quencheth the light of the heart, and extinguisheth the life of the soul.

223   HOW COULDST THOU FORGET thine own faults and busy thyself with the faults of others? Whoso doeth this is accursed of Me.

224   BREATHE NOT the sins of others so long as thou art thyself a sinner. Shouldst thou transgress this command, accursed wouldst thou be, and to this I bear witness.

225   HEAR NO EVIL, and see no evil, abase not thyself, neither sigh and weep. Speak no evil, that thou mayest not hear it spoken unto thee, and magnify not the faults of others, that thine own faults may not appear great; and wish not the abasement of anyone, that thine own abasement be not exposed. Live then the days of thy life, that are less than a fleeting moment, with thy mind stainless, thy heart unsullied, thy thoughts pure, and thy nature sanctified, so that, free and content, thou mayest put away this mortal frame, and repair unto the mystic paradise and abide in the eternal kingdom for evermore.

> *Material fire consumeth the body, whereas the fire of the tongue devoureth both heart and soul. The force of the former lasteth but for a time, whilst the effects of the latter endure a century.*

226   The tongue I have designed for the mention of Me, defile it not with detraction. If the fire of self overcome you, remember your own faults and not the faults of My creatures, inasmuch as every one of you knoweth his own self better than he knoweth others.

227   How blessed are these aims, especially the prevention of backbiting! I hope that you may become confirmed therein, because the worst human quality *and the most great sin is backbiting*, more especially when it emanates from the tongues of the believers of God. If some means were devised so that the doors of backbiting were shut eternally and each one of the believers unsealed his lips in praise of others, then the Teachings of His Holiness Bahá'u'lláh would spread, the hearts illumined, the spirits glorified, and the human world would attain to everlasting felicity.

   I hope that the believers of God will shun completely backbiting, each one praising the other cordially and believe that backbiting is the cause of Divine wrath, to such an extent that if a person backbites to the extent of one word, he may become dishonoured among all the people, because the most hateful characteristic of man is fault-finding. One must expose the praiseworthy qualities of the souls and not their evil attributes. The friends must overlook their shortcomings and faults and speak only of their virtues and not their defects.

   ... This is the attribute of the children of the Kingdom. This is the conduct and the manner of the real Bahá'ís. I hope that all the believers will attain to this lofty station.

228   As REGARDS BACKBITING, i.e. discussing the faults of others in their absence, the teachings are very emphatic. In a Tablet to an American friend the Master wrote: 'The worst human quality and the most great sin is backbiting, more especially when it emanates from the tongues of the believers of God. If some means were devised so that the doors of backbiting were shut eternally and each one of the believers unsealed his lips in praise of others, then the Teachings of His Holiness Bahá'u'lláh would spread, the hearts be illumined, the spirits glorified, and the human world would attain to everlasting felicity.' …Bahá'u'lláh says in [The] Hidden Words: 'Breathe not the sins of others so long as thou art a sinner. Shouldst thou transgress this command ACCURSED ART THOU.' The condemnation of backbiting could hardly be couched in stronger language than in these passages, and it is obviously one of the foremost obligations for Bahá'ís to set their faces against this practice. Even if what is said against another person be true, the mentioning of his faults to others still comes under the category of backbiting, and is forbidden.

229   THE QUESTION of dealing with those who call themselves Bahá'ís but who act in ways which we believe to be detrimental to the interests of the Cause is a very difficult one. If we think we can help matters by a frank and friendly talk with the individual concerned, refraining from judging or condemning, but pointing out in as kind a manner as possible the way in which, as it seems to us, the sort of conduct in question is harmful to the Cause or of a nature forbidden by the teachings, then it seems well to try that method before resorting to the more formidable method of bringing the matter before the Spiritual Assembly. But if that fails or if we feel that it is hopeless to try and deal with the matter in that way, while at the same time the case is so serious that the

One must expose the praiseworthy qualities of the souls and not their evil attributes. The friends must overlook their shortcomings and faults and speak only of their virtues and not their defects.

interests of the Cause require that it should be firmly dealt with, then the proper course is to bring the matter before the Spiritual Assembly and have it frankly and fully discussed, calling such evidence as is necessary for the elucidation of the matter. After full consideration, the Spiritual Assembly should take such action as it deems advisable, and it is incumbent upon all members of the group to be loyal to whatever decision is arrived at by the Spiritual Assembly. There is, of course the right of appeal from the Local to the National Assembly, and from that to Shoghi Effendi,* but the matter ought to be dealt with, in the first instance, by the Local Spiritual Assembly.

...When a difficulty is brought out into the daylight and freely discussed by a duly authorised and responsible group of people who are sincerely desirous of finding the best solution and are free from prejudice or personal motive, then there is a good chance of overcoming it, but discussions of and faults [sic] of others, behind their backs, by unauthorised people who have no authority to take action in the matter, is surely one of the most fertile causes – probably THE most fertile cause – of disunity, and the importance of putting an end to this practice should be impressed on all Bahá'ís.

230 IT IS OBVIOUS that if we listen to those who complain to us about the faults of others we are guilty of complicity in their backbiting. We should therefore, as tactfully as possible, but yet firmly, do our utmost to prevent others from making accusations or complaints against others in our presence.

---

* Today to the Universal House of Justice

231   I F WE BAHÁ'ÍS cannot attain to cordial unity among ourselves, then we fail to realize the main purpose for which the Báb, Bahá'u'lláh and the Beloved Master lived and suffered. In order to achieve this cordial unity one of the first essentials insisted on by Bahá'u'lláh and 'Abdu'l-Bahá is that we resist the natural tendency to let our attention dwell on the faults and failings of others rather than on our own. Each of us is responsible for one life only, and that is our own. Each of us is immeasurably far from being 'perfect as our heavenly Father is perfect' and the task of perfecting our own life and character is one that requires all our attention, our will-power and energy. If we allow our attention and energy to be taken up in efforts to keep others right and remedy their faults, we are wasting precious time. We are like ploughmen each of whom has his team to manage and his plough to direct, and in order to keep his furrow straight he must keep his eye on his goal and concentrate on his own task. If he looks to this side and that to see how Tom and Harry are getting on and to criticise their ploughing, then his furrow will assuredly become crooked. On no subject are the Bahá'í teachings more emphatic than on the necessity to abstain from fault-finding and backbiting while being ever eager to discover and root out our own faults and overcome our own failings.

232   WHAT THE BELIEVERS need is not only, as you state, to really study the teachings, but also to have more peace-makers circulating among them. Unfortunately, not only average people, but average Bahá'ís, are very immature; gossip, trouble-making, criticism, seem easier than the putting into practice of love, constructive words and cooperation. It is one of the functions of the older and the more mature Bahá'ís, to help the weaker ones to iron out their difficulties and learn to really function and live like true believers!

> *On no subject are the Bahá'í teachings more emphatic than on the necessity to abstain from fault-finding and backbiting while being ever eager to discover and root out our own faults and overcome our own failings.*

233   W<small>HEN CRITICISM AND HARSH WORDS</small> arise within a Bahá'í community, there is no remedy except to put the past behind one, and persuade all concerned to turn over a new leaf, and for the sake of God and His Faith refrain from mentioning the subjects which have led to misunderstanding and inharmony. The more the friends argue back and forth and maintain, each side, that their point of view is the right one the worse the whole situation becomes.

    When we see the condition the world is in today, we must surely forget these utterly insignificant internal disturbances, and rush, unitedly, to the rescue of humanity. You should urge your fellow Bahá'ís to take this point of view, and to support you in a strong effort to suppress every critical thought and every harsh word, in order to let the spirit of Bahá'u'lláh flow into the entire community, and unite it in His love and in His service.

234   Y<small>OU ASK</small> in your letter for guidance on the implications of the prohibition on backbiting and more specifically whether, in moments of anger or depression, the believer is permitted to turn to his friends to unburden his soul and discuss his problem in human relations. Normally, it is possible to describe the situation surrounding a problem and seek help and advice in resolving it, without necessarily mentioning names. The individual believer should seek to do this, whether he is consulting a friend, Bahá'í or non-Bahá'í, or whether the friend is consulting him.

    'Abdu'l-Bahá does not permit adverse criticism of individuals by name in discussion among the friends, even if the one criticizing believes that he is doing so to protect the interests of the Cause. If the situation is of such gravity as to endanger the interests of the Faith, the complaint, as your National Spiritual Assembly has indicated, should be submitted to the Local Spiritual Assembly, or as you state to a representative of the institution of the Counsellors, for consideration and action. In such cases, of course, the name of the person or persons involved will have to be mentioned.

You also ask what one should do to 'handle depression and anger with someone' one feels 'very positively about'. The Universal House of Justice suggests that you call to mind the admonitions found in our Writings on the need to overlook the shortcomings of others, to forgive and conceal their misdeeds, not to expose their bad qualities, but to search for and affirm their praiseworthy ones, and endeavour to be always forbearing, patient, and merciful.

235   As to backbiting, the House of Justice points out that learning not to concern oneself with the faults of others seems to be one of the most difficult lessons for people to master, and that failing in this is a fertile cause of disputes among Bahá'ís as it is among men and women in general. In Star of the West, Volume 8, No. 10, on page 138, there is a record of a reply given by 'Abdu'l-Bahá in a private interview in Paris in 1913. He was asked 'How shall I overcome seeing the faults of others – recognizing the wrong in others?', and He replied: 'I will tell you. Whenever you recognize the fault of another, think of yourself! What are my imperfections? – and try to remove them. Do this whenever you are tried through the words or deeds of others. Thus you will grow, become more perfect. You will overcome self, you will not even have time to think of the faults of others . . .' You are quite correct in your understanding of the importance of avoiding backbiting; such conduct strikes at the very unity of the Bahá'í community. In a letter written to an individual believer on behalf of the Guardian it is stated: 'If we are better, if we show love, patience, and

> *Whenever you recognize the fault of another, think of yourself! What are my imperfections? – and try to remove them. Do this whenever you are tried through the words or deeds of others. Thus you will grow, become more perfect. You will overcome self, you will not even have time to think of the faults of others . . .*

understanding of the weakness of others, if we seek to never criticize but rather encourage, others will do likewise, and we can really help the Cause through our example and spiritual strength.'

13

'Behold Me Standing Before Your Face …'

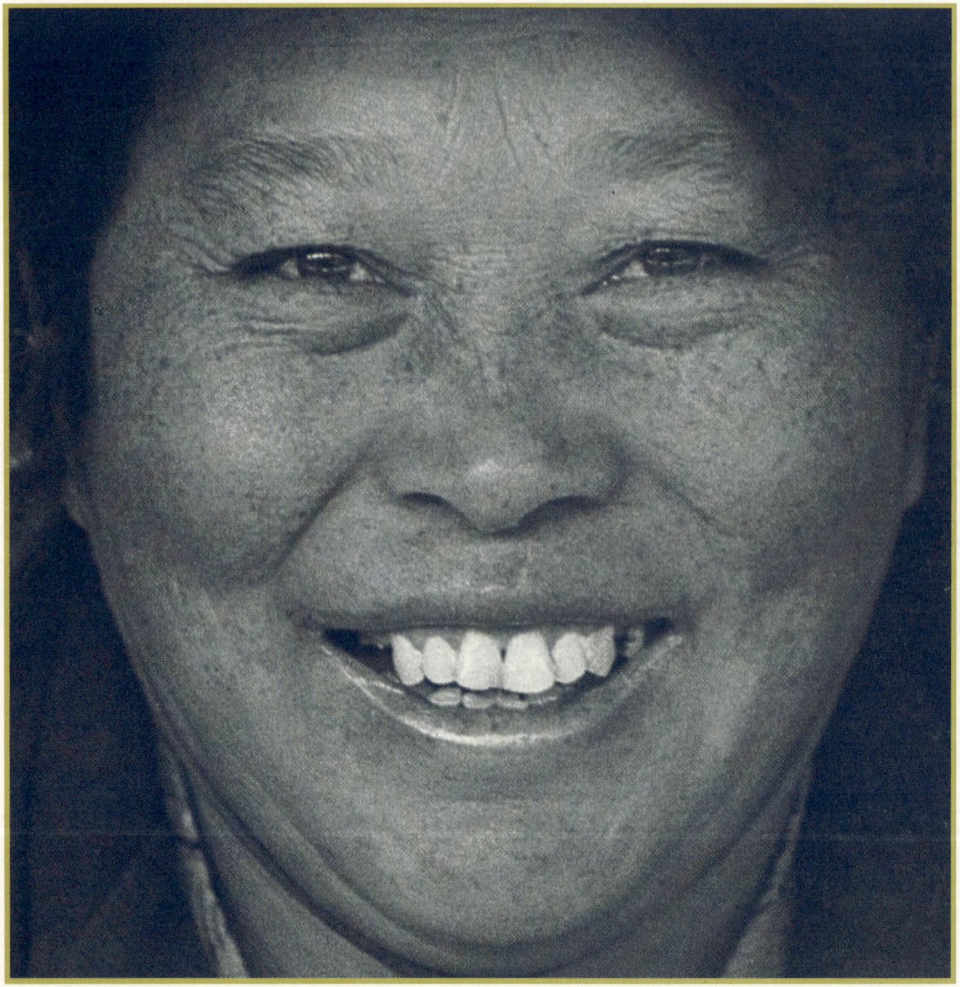

236   It is Our wish and desire that every one of you may become a source of all goodness unto men, and an example of uprightness to mankind. Beware lest ye prefer yourselves above your neighbours. Fix your gaze upon Him Who is the Temple of God amongst men. He, in truth hath offered up His life as a ransom for the redemption of the world. He, verily, is the All-Bountiful, the Gracious, the Most High. If any differences arise amongst you, behold Me standing before your face, and overlook the faults of one another for My name's sake and as a token of your love for My manifest and resplendent Cause. We love to see you at all times consorting in amity and concord within the paradise of My good-pleasure; and to inhale from your acts the fragrance of friendliness and unity, of loving-kindness and fellowship. Thus counselleth you the All-Knowing, the Faithful. We shall always be with you; if We inhale the perfume of your fellowship, Our heart will assuredly rejoice, for naught else can satisfy Us. To this beareth witness every man of true understanding.

237   ✦ ✦ ✦ The Cause of the Ancient Beauty is the very essence of love, the very channel of oneness, existing only that all may become the waves of one sea, and bright stars of the same endless sky, and pearls within the shell of singleness, and gleaming jewels quarried from the mines of unity; that they may become servants one to another, bless one another, praise one another; that each one may loose his tongue and extol the rest without exception, each one voice his gratitude to all the rest; that all should lift up their eyes to the horizon of glory, and remember that they are linked to the Holy Threshold; that they should see nothing but good in one another, hear nothing but praise of one another, and speak no word of one another save only to praise.

> *If any differences arise amongst you, behold Me standing before your face, and overlook the faults of one another for My name's sake and as a token of your love for My manifest and resplendent Cause.*

There are indeed certain ones who tread this way of righteousness, and God be thanked, these are strengthened and supported by heavenly power in every land. But others have not arisen as they ought to this gloried and exalted station, and this doth lay upon the heart of 'Abdu'l-Bahá a heavy burden of grief, of inconceivable grief. For no tempest more perilous than this could ever assail the Cause of God, nor could anything else so diminish the influence of His Word.

It behoveth all the beloved of God to become as one, to gather together under the protection of a single flag, to stand for a uniform body of opinion, to follow one and the same pathway, to hold fast to a single resolve. Let them forget their divergent theories and put aside their conflicting views since, God be praised, our purpose is one, our goal is one. We are the servants of one Threshold; we all are gathered in the shade of the same high Tabernacle, we all are sheltered under the one celestial Tree.

O beloved of the Lord! If any soul speak ill of an absent one, the only result will clearly be this; he will dampen the zeal of the friends and tend to make them indifferent. For backbiting is divisive, it is the leading cause among the friends of a disposition to withdraw. If any individual should speak ill of one who is absent, it is incumbent on his hearers, in a spiritual and friendly manner, to stop him, and say in effect: would this detraction serve any useful purpose? Would it please the Blessed Beauty, contribute to the lasting honour of the friends, promote the holy Faith, support the Covenant, or be of any possible benefit to any soul? No, never! On the contrary, it would make the dust to settle so thickly on the heart that the ears would hear no more, and the eyes would no longer behold the light of truth.

If however, a person setteth about speaking well of another, opening his lips to praise another, he will touch an answering chord in his hearers and they will be stirred up by the breathings of God. Their hearts and souls will rejoice to know that, God be thanked, here is a soul in the Faith who is a focus of human perfections, a very embodiment of the bounties of the Lord; one whose tongue is eloquent, and whose face shineth, in whatever gathering he may be, one who hath victory upon his brow, and who is a being sustained by the sweet savours of God.

Now which is the better way? I swear this by the beauty of the Lord: whensoever I hear good of the friends, my heart filleth up with joy; but whensoever I find even a hint that they are on bad terms one with another, I am overwhelmed by grief. Such is the condition of 'Abdu'l-Bahá. Then judge from this where your duty lieth.

238 I BESEECH YOU, one and all, to add your prayers to mine to the end that war and bloodshed may cease, and that love, friendship, peace and unity may reign in the world.

239 O HOW I LONG to see the loved ones taking upon themselves the responsibilities of the Cause! Now is the time to proclaim the Kingdom of Bahá! Now is the hour of love and union! This is the day of the spiritual harmony of the loved ones of God! All the resources of my physical strength I have exhausted, and the spirit of my life is the welcome tidings of the unity of the people of Bahá. I am straining my ears toward the East and toward the West, toward the North and toward the South that haply I may hear the songs of love and fellowship chanted in the meetings of the faithful. My days are numbered, and, but for this, there is no joy left unto me. O how I yearn to see the friends united even as a string of gleaming pearls, as the brilliant Pleiades, as the rays of the sun, as the gazelles of one meadow!

I beseech you, one and all, to add your prayers to mine to the end that war and bloodshed may cease, and that love, friendship, peace and unity may reign in the world.

The mystic Nightingale is warbling for them all; will they not listen? The Bird of Paradise is singing; will they not heed? The angel of Abhá is calling to them; will they not hearken? The Herald of the Covenant is pleading; will they not obey? Ah me, I am waiting, waiting to hear the joyful tidings that the believers are the very embodiment of sincerity and truthfulness, the incarnation of love and amity, the living symbols of unity and concord. Will they not gladden my heart? Will they not satisfy my yearning? Will they not manifest my wish? Will they not fulfil my heart's desire? Will they not give ear to my call?

I am waiting, I am patiently waiting.

References

Chapter 1

1. Bahá'u'lláh, Lawḥ-i-Maqṣúd ('Tablet of Maqṣúd'), *Tablets of Bahá'u'lláh revealed after the Kitáb-i-Aqdas*, comp. Research Department of the Universal House of Justice, trans. Habib Taherzadeh and others, 1st pocket-sized ed. (Wilmette, Ill: 1988) p. 167.
2. Bahá'u'lláh, *Gleanings from the Writings of Bahá'u'lláh*, comp. and trans. Shoghi Effendi, rev. ed. (London: Bahá'í Publishing Trust, 1978) XXXIV, p. 81.
3. Bahá'u'lláh, ibid., CXI, p. 216.
4. Bahá'u'lláh, Ishráqát ('Splendours'), *Tablets*, pp. 127-8.
5. 'Abdu'l-Bahá, *The Promulgation of Universal Peace; Talks Delivered by 'Abdu'l-Bahá during His Visit to the United States and Canada in 1912*, comp. Howard MacNutt, 2nd ed. (Wilmette, Ill: Bahá'í Publishing Trust, 1982) p. 297.
6. 'Abdu'l-Bahá, *Paris Talks; Addresses Given By 'Abdu'l-Bahá in Paris in 1911-1912*, 11th ed. (London: Bahá'í Publishing Trust, 1971) pp. 129-30.
7. 'Abdu'l-Bahá, ibid., p. 129.
8. 'Abdu'l-Bahá, *Promulgation*, p. 287.
9. 'Abdu'l-Bahá, *Selections from the Writings of 'Abdu'l-Bahá*, comp. Research Department of the Universal House of Justice, trans. Marzieh Gail and others, rev. ed. (Haifa: Bahá'í World Centre, 1982) 15, pp. 31-2.
10. Shoghi Effendi, letter dated 11 March 1936 'To the beloved of God and the handmaids of the Merciful throughout the West', published as 'The Unfoldment of World Civilization', *The World Order of Bahá'u'lláh; Selected Letters*, 1st pocket-size ed. (Wilmette, Ill: Bahá'í Publishing Trust, 1991) p. 202.
11. The Universal House of Justice, *The Promise of World Peace; A Statement by the Universal House of Justice*, rev. ed. (London: Bahá'í Publishing Trust, 1992) p. 17
12. The Universal House of Justice, ibid., p. 22.

Chapter 2

13. Bahá'u'lláh, *Consultation*, comp. Research Department of the Universal House of Justice, rev. ed. (London: Bahá'í Publishing Trust, 1990) p. 1.
14. Bahá'u'lláh, *Gleanings*, CXXXII, p. 287.
15. Bahá'u'lláh, CXII, p. 217.
16. Bahá'u'lláh, Bishárát ('Glad Tidings'), *Tablets*, p. 22.
17. Bahá'u'lláh, *Gleanings*, CXII, p. 217.
18. Bahá'u'lláh, *The Hidden Words*, trans. Shoghi Effendi, 'with the assistance of some English friends' (London: Nightingale Books, 1992) p. 29.
19. Bahá'u'lláh, *Gleanings*, CXI, p. 216.
20. Bahá'u'lláh, Bishárát, *Tablets*, p. 22.
21. 'Abdu'l-Bahá, *Selections*, 225, p. 286.
22. 'Abdu'l-Bahá, *Paris Talks*, p. 29.
23. 'Abdu'l-Bahá, *Promulgation*, p. 300.
24. 'Abdu'l-Bahá, ibid., p. 287.
25. 'Abdu'l-Bahá, *Paris Talks*, p. 136.
26. 'Abdu'l-Bahá, *Promulgation*, p. 300.
27. 'Abdu'l-Bahá, *Paris Talks*, p.53.
28. Shoghi Effendi, letter dated 28 March 1941 to 'Friends and fellow-heirs of the Kingdom of Bahá'u'lláh', published as *The Promised Day is Come*, rev. ed. (Wilmette, Ill: Bahá'í Publishing Trust, 1980) pp. 122-3.
29. Shoghi Effendi, *The World Order of Bahá'u'lláh*, p. 204.
30. Shoghi Effendi, ibid., p. 136.
31. The Universal House of Justice, *The Promise of World Peace*, p. 16.
32. The Universal House of Justice, ibid., p. 21.

Chapter 3

33. 'Abdu'l-Bahá, *Paris Talks*, p. 139.
34. 'Abdu'l-Bahá, *Selections*, 15, p. 31.
35. 'Abdu'l-Bahá, *Paris Talks*, p. 139.
36. 'Abdu'l-Bahá, *Promulgation*, p. 150.
37. 'Abdu'l-Bahá, *Selections*, 225, p. 289.
38. 'Abdu'l-Bahá, ibid., p. 290.
39. 'Abdu'l-Bahá, *Promulgation*, p. 321.
40. 'Abdu'l-Bahá, *Selections*, p. 278.
41. 'Abdu'l-Bahá, *Promulgation*, p. 57

Chapter 4

42. 'Abdu'l-Bahá, attached to a letter dated 4 February 1985, written on behalf of the Universal House of Justice to the National Spiritual Assembly of the Bahá'ís of the United States, *The Power of Unity; Beyond Prejudice and Racism*, comp. Bonnie J. Taylor, National Race Unity Committee, Bahá'í Publishing Trust (Wilmette, Ill: Bahá'í Publishing Trust, 1986) p. 69.
43. 'Abdu'l-Bahá, *Promulgation*, p. 425.
44. 'Abdu'l-Bahá, quoted by Shoghi Effendi in a letter dated 25 December 1938, 'To the beloved of God and the handmaids of the Merciful throughout the United States and Canada', published as *The Advent of Divine Justice*, 1st pocket-sized ed. (Wilmette, Ill: Bahá'í Publishing Trust, 1990) p. 37.
45. 'Abdu'l-Bahá, *Promulgation*, p. 427.
46. 'Abdu'l-Bahá, ibid., pp. 67-8.
47. 'Abdu'l-Bahá, *Paris Talks*, p. 148.
48. 'Abdu'l-Bahá, attached to a letter dated 4 February 1985, written on behalf of the Universal House of Justice to the National Spiritual Assembly of the Bahá'ís of the United States, *The Power of Unity*, p. 31.
49. Shoghi Effendi, *The Advent of Divine Justice*, p. 35.
50. Written on behalf of Shoghi Effendi, letter dated 27 May 1957 to the Bahá'í Inter-Racial Teaching Committee, Gayle Morrison, *To Move the World; Louis G. Gregory and the Advancement of Racial Unity in America* (Wilmette, Ill: Bahá'í Publishing Trust, 1982) p. 294.
51. The Universal House of Justice, *The Promise of World Peace*, p. 12.

Chapter 5

52 Bahá'u'lláh, *Gleanings*, CVII, p. 213.
53 Bahá'u'lláh, Is͟hráqát, *Tablets*, p. 129.
54 Bahá'u'lláh, *Gleanings*, XXXIV, p. 79.
55 Bahá'u'lláh, *Epistle to the Son of the Wolf*, trans. Shoghi Effendi (Wilmette, Ill: Bahá'í Publishing Trust, 1st pocket-sized ed, 1988) p. 12.
56 Bahá'u'lláh, quoted in Shoghi Effendi, *The World Order of Bahá'u'lláh*, p. 186.
57 'Abdu'l-Bahá, *Promulgation*, pp. 338-9.
58 'Abdu'l-Bahá, '*Abdu'l-Bahá in London; Addresses and Notes of Conversations*, comp. and ed. Eric Hammond (London: Bahá'í Publishing Trust, 1982 ed.), pp. 19-20.
59 'Abdu'l-Bahá, *Selections*, 8, p. 24.
60 'Abdu'l-Bahá, ibid., 225, pp. 291-2.
61 'Abdu'l-Bahá, ibid., 225, p. 292.
62 'Abdu'l-Bahá, *The Secret of Divine Civilization*, trans. Marzieh Gail, 1st pocket-sized ed. (Wilmette, Ill: Bahá'í Publishing Trust, 1990) p. 73.
63 'Abdu'l-Bahá, *Paris Talks*, p. 129.
64 'Abdu'l-Bahá, *Promulgation*, p. 370.
65 'Abdu'l-Bahá, *Paris Talks*, p. 38.
66 'Abdu'l-Bahá, ibid., p. 129.
67 'Abdu'l-Bahá, *Promulgation*, pp. 108-9.
68 'Abdu'l-Bahá, ibid., p. 129.
69 'Abdu'l-Bahá, ibid., pp. 129-30.
70 'Abdu'l-Bahá, ibid., p. 321.
71 'Abdu'l-Bahá, ibid.
72 'Abdu'l-Bahá, ibid., p. 392.
73 'Abdu'l-Bahá, *The Secret of Divine Civilization*, p. 73.
74 'Abdu'l-Bahá, *Promulgation*, p. 151.
75 'Abdu'l-Bahá, ibid., p. 391.
76 'Abdu'l-Bahá, *Selections*, 15, p. 31.
77 'Abdu'l-Bahá, *Promulgation*, p. 90.
78 'Abdu'l-Bahá, *Selections*, 15, p. 30.
79 'Abdu'l-Bahá, ibid., 31, p. 63.
80 Shoghi Effendi, letter dated 28 November 1931 'To fellow-believers in the Faith of Bahá'u'lláh', published as 'The goal of a New World Order', *The World Order of Bahá'u'lláh*, p. 198.

Chapter 6

81 Bahá'u'lláh, *Epistle*, p. 62.
82 Bahá'u'lláh, *Gleanings*, CXXXI, p. 285.
83 Bahá'u'lláh, ibid., XLIII, p. 97.
84 Bahá'u'lláh, ibid., IV, p. 6.
85 Bahá'u'lláh, Law͟h-i-Dunyá ('Tablet of the World'), *Tablets*, p. 87.
86 Bahá'u'lláh, *Epistle*, p. 24.
87 'Abdu'l-Bahá, *Paris Talks*, p. 54.
88 'Abdu'l-Bahá, *Promulgation*, p. 174.
89 'Abdu'l-Bahá, *Paris Talks*, p. 140.
90 'Abdu'l-Bahá, *Promulgation*, p. 449.
91 'Abdu'l-Bahá, *The Will and Testament of 'Abdu'l-Bahá*, trans. Shoghi Effendi, (Wilmette, Ill: Bahá'í Publishing Trust, 1968), p. 13.
92 'Abdu'l-Bahá, *Selections*, 7, p. 20.
93 'Abdu'l-Bahá, ibid., pp. 19-20.
94 Shoghi Effendi, *The World Order of Bahá'u'lláh*, pp. 41-2.
95 Shoghi Effendi, ibid., pp. 42-3.
96 Shoghi Effendi, ibid., p. 43.
97 Shoghi Effendi, ibid., p. 201.
98 Shoghi Effendi, ibid., p. 203.
99 The Universal House of Justice, letter dated 13 July 1972 to all National Spiritual Assemblies, *Messages From The Universal House of Justice 1968-1973* (Wilmette, Ill: Bahá'í Publishing Trust, 1976), p. 100.
100 The Universal House of Justice, letter dated 8 December 1967 to an individual, *The Power of Unity*, p. 44.
101 The Universal House of Justice, message dated 20 October 1983 to the Bahá'ís of the World, *A Wider Horizon; Selected Messages of the Universal House of Justice 1983-1992* (Riviera Beach, Fl: Palabra Publications, 1992) p. 7.
102 The Universal House of Justice, letter dated 29 December 1988, to the followers of Bahá'u'lláh in the United States of America, published as *Individual Rights and Freedoms in the World Order of Bahá'u'lláh* (Wilmette, Ill: Bahá'í Publishing Trust, 1989) p. 21.
103 The Universal House of Justice, ibid., pp. 21-2.

Chapter 7

104 Bahá'u'lláh, *Gleanings*, CX, p. 214
105 Bahá'u'lláh, *Divorce; Extracts from the Bahá'í Teachings Discouraging Divorce*, comp. Research Department of the Universal House of Justice. (London: Bahá'í Publishing Trust, 1986) p. 5.
106 Bahá'u'lláh, Is͟hráqát, *Tablets*, p. 129.
107 Bahá'u'lláh, *Gleanings*, XCVI, pp. 195-6.
108 Bahá'u'lláh, Law͟h-i-Dunyá, *Tablets*, p. 88.
109 Bahá'u'lláh, Kitáb-i-'Ahd ('Book of the Covenant'), ibid., p. 222.
110 Bahá'u'lláh, quoted in a letter from the Universal House of Justice to all National Spiritual Assemblies, 27 March 1978.
111 The Báb, Kitáb-i-Asmá' ('The Book of Names'), *Selections from the Writings of the Báb*, comp. Research Department of the Universal House of Justice, trans. Habib Taherzadeh with the assistance of a Committee at the Bahá'í World Centre (Haifa: Bahá'í World Centre, 1978) p. 129.
112 The Báb, Qayyúmu'l-Asmá', ibid., p. 156.
113 'Abdu'l-Bahá, *Paris Talks*, pp. 180-1.
114 'Abdu'l-Bahá, *Promulgation*, p. 156.
115 'Abdu'l-Bahá, ibid., p. 190.
116 'Abdu'l-Bahá, *Bahá'í World Faith; Selected Writings of Bahá'u'lláh and 'Abdu'l-Bahá* (Wilmette, Ill: Bahá'í Publishing Trust, 1956 ed.) pp. 402-3.
117 'Abdu'l-Bahá, *Selections*, 174, p. 203.
118 Ibid.
119 Ibid., 221, p. 280.
120 'Abdu'l-Bahá, *Promulgation*, p. 24.
121 'Abdu'l-Bahá, *Selections*, 221, p. 277.
122 'Abdu'l-Bahá, ibid., 36, p. 76.
123 'Abdu'l-Bahá, *Promulgation*, p. 93.
124 'Abdu'l-Bahá, *Selections*, 42, p. 86.
125 Shoghi Effendi, *The Advent of Divine Justice*, p. 35.
126 Written on behalf of Shoghi Effendi, letter dated 17 February 1947 to an

individual, *Living the Life; Being two compilations; the first of guidance given by the Guardian and the second of guidance given by the Universal House of Justice* (London: Bahá'í Publishing Trust, 1974) pp. 26-7.
127 Written on behalf of Shoghi Effendi, letter dated 26 December 1941 to the National Spiritual Assembly of the Bahá'ís of Australia and New Zealand, ibid., p. 18.
128 The Universal House of Justice, letter dated 13 July 1972 to all National Spiritual Assemblies, *Messages From The Universal House of Justice*, pp. 99-100.

Chapter 8

129 Bahá'u'lláh, *Gleanings*, CXXXII, pp. 287-8.
130 Bahá'u'lláh, Tarázát ('Ornaments'), *Tablets*, p. 36.
131 Bahá'u'lláh, Lawh-i-Dunyá, ibid., p. 88.
132 Bahá'u'lláh, *Gleanings*, CLVI, pp. 332-3.
133 'Abdu'l-Bahá, *Selections*, 39, p. 81.
134 'Abdu'l-Bahá, ibid., 7, pp. 20-1.
135 'Abdu'l-Bahá, ibid., p. 21.
136 'Abdu'l-Bahá, ibid., p. 20.
137 'Abdu'l-Bahá, ibid., 8, p. 24.
138 'Abdu'l-Bahá, ibid., 7, p. 20.
139 'Abdu'l-Bahá, *Paris Talks*, p. 170.
140 'Abdu'l-Bahá, *Selections*, 34, p. 69.
141 'Abdu'l-Bahá, *Will and Testament*, p. 14.
142 'Abdu'l-Bahá, *Promulgation*, p. 291.
143 'Abdu'l-Bahá, ibid., p. 420.
144 'Abdu'l-Bahá, *Paris Talks*, p. 87.
145 'Abdu'l-Bahá, *Selections*, 17, p. 36.
146 Written on behalf of Shoghi Effendi, letter dated 5 May 1943 to an individual, *The Power of Unity*, p. 99.
147 Written on behalf of Shoghi Effendi, letter dated 20 October 1945 to an individual, *Living the Life*, pp. 23-4.
148 Written on behalf of Shoghi Effendi, letter dated 14 February 1925 to an individual, ibid., p. 9.
149 The Universal House of Justice, message to the Bahá'ís of the World, Riḍván 1988, *A Wider Horizon*, pp. 56-7.
150 The Universal House of Justice, letter dated 8 December 1967 to an individual, *Wellspring of Guidance; Messages 1963–1968* (Wilmette, Ill: Bahá'í Publishing Trust, 1970), pp. 133–4.
151 The Universal House of Justice, *The Promise of World Peace*, pp. 22-3.

Chapter 9

152 'Abdu'l-Bahá, *Promulgation*, pp. 445-6.
153 'Abdu'l-Bahá, *Selections*, 183, pp. 208-9.
154 'Abdu'l-Bahá, ibid., 186, p. 215.
155 'Abdu'l-Bahá, *Promulgation*, p. 381.
156 'Abdu'l-Bahá, quoted in Shoghi Effendi, *God Passes By*, rev. ed. (Wilmette, Ill: Bahá'í Publishing Trust, 1974), p. 238.
157 'Abdu'l-Bahá, ibid., p. 239
158 'Abdu'l-Bahá, *Selections*, 192, p. 228
159 'Abdu'l-Bahá, *The Covenant*, comp. Research Department of the Universal House of Justice (London: Bahá'í Publishing Trust, 1988) p. 17.
160 The Universal House of Justice, *The Constitution of the Universal House of Justice* (Haifa: Bahá'í World Centre, 1972), pp. 3-4.
161 The Universal House of Justice, *Individual Rights and Freedoms*, p. 16.
162 The Universal House of Justice, message dated 26 November 1992 to the Bahá'ís of the world, *The Holy Year 1992-1993* (Riviera Beach Fl: Palabra Publications, 1993) pp. 35-6.
163 The Universal House of Justice, ibid., pp. 38-9.
164 The Universal House of Justice, letter dated 3 January 1982 to an individual, *The Covenant*, p. 18.

Chapter 10

165 'Abdu'l-Bahá, *Selections*, 92, p. 122.
166 'Abdu'l-Bahá, *Preserving Bahá'í Marriages; A Memorandum and Compilation Prepared by the Research Department of the Universal House of Justice*, comp. Research Department of the Universal House of Justice (London: Bahá'í Publishing Trust, 1991) p. 17.
167 Written on behalf of Shoghi Effendi, letter dated 20 January 1943 to an individual, *Family Life*, comp. Research Department of the Universal House of Justice (London: Bahá'í Publishing Trust, 1982) pp. 21-2.
168 Written on behalf of Shoghi Effendi, letter dated 25 October 1947 to the National Spiritual Assembly of the Bahá'ís of the United States, ibid., pp. 23-4.
169 Written on behalf of Shoghi Effendi, letter dated 6 June 1954 to an individual, ibid., p. 26.
170 'Abdu'l-Bahá, *Selections*, 221, p. 279.
171 'Abdu'l-Bahá, *Promulgation*, p. 136.
172 Written on behalf of Shoghi Effendi, letter dated 16 November 1936 to an individual, *Divorce*, p. 9.
173 Written on behalf of Shoghi Effendi, letter dated 6 July 1952 to an individual, *Family Life*, p. 25.
174 Written on behalf of Shoghi Effendi, letter dated 9 November 1956 to the National Spiritual Assembly of the Bahá'ís of Central America, ibid., pp. 27-8.
175 The Universal House of Justice, letter dated 28 December 1980 to the National Spiritual Assembly of the Bahá'ís of New Zealand, ibid., p. 30.
176 Bahá'u'lláh, *The Kitáb-i-Aqdas; The Most Holy Book*, rev. ed. (London: Bahá'í Publishing Trust, 1993) 57, p. 40.
177 'Abdu'l-Bahá, *The Nineteen Day Feast*, comp. Research Department of the Universal House of Justice (London: Bahá'í Publishing Trust, 1989) p. 1.
178 'Abdu'l-Bahá, ibid.
179 'Abdu'l-Bahá, ibid., p. 3.
180 'Abdu'l-Bahá, *Star of the West* (Oxford: George Ronald, bound vols, 1978), vol. 4, no. 7 (13 July 1913), p. 120.
181 Ibid.
182 'Abdu'l-Bahá, *The Nineteen Day Feast*, p. 5.
183 'Abdu'l-Bahá, ibid., p. 5.
184 'Abdu'l-Bahá, *Tablets of Abdul Baha Abbas* (Chicago: Bahá'í Publishing Society, 1915) vol. 2, p. 553.
185 The Universal House of Justice, letter dated 27 August 1989 to the Bahá'ís of the World, *The Nineteen Day Feast*, p. v.
186 The Universal House of Justice, ibid., p. vii.
187 'Abdu'l-Bahá, *Star of the West*, vol. 8, no. 9, 20 August 1917, p. 114.

188 'Abdu'l-Bahá, *Consultation*, p. 6.
189 'Abdu'l-Bahá, quoted in a letter by Shoghi Effendi dated 5 March 1922 to 'fellow-workers in the Cause of Bahá'u'lláh', *Bahá'í Administration*, 5th rev. ed. (Wilmette, Ill: Bahá'í Publishing Trust, 1968) pp. 21-2.
190 'Abdu'l-Bahá, *Promulgation*, p. 72.
191 'Abdu'l-Bahá, quoted in Shoghi Effendi, *Bahá'í Administration*, pp. 22-3.
192 Shoghi Effendi, letter dated 29 January 1925 to the National Spiritual Assembly of the United States and Canada, ibid., p. 80.
193 Written on behalf of Shoghi Effendi, letter dated 28 October 1935 to an individual.
194 Written on behalf of Shoghi Effendi, letter dated 18 April 1939 to an individual.
195 Written on behalf of Shoghi Effendi, letter dated 19 October 1947 to an individual.
196 The Universal House of Justice, letter dated 6 March 1970 to the National Spiritual Assembly of Canada.
197 Written on behalf of the Universal House of Justice, letter dated 25 December 1983 to an individual.
198 Written on behalf of the Universal House of Justice, letter dated 20 December 1987 to the National Spiritual Assembly of the Bahá'ís of the United States.

Chapter 11

199 Bahá'u'lláh, *Gleanings*, LXXII, p. 139.
200 Bahá'u'lláh, ibid., V, pp. 8-9.
201 'Abdu'l-Bahá, *The Secret of Divine Civilization*, p. 53.
202 Written on behalf of Shoghi Effendi, letter dated 24 September 1933 to an individual, *Living the Life*, p. 13.
203 Written on behalf of Shoghi Effendi, letter dated 23 August 1939 to an individual, ibid., p. 17.
204 Written on behalf of Shoghi Effendi, letter dated 27 February 1943 to an individual, ibid., pp. 18-19.
205 Written on behalf of Shoghi Effendi, letter dated 17 March 1943 to an individual.
206 Written on behalf of Shoghi Effendi, letter dated 26 October 1943 to an individual.
207 Written on behalf of Shoghi Effendi, letter dated 26 October 1943 to the National Spiritual Assembly of the Bahá'ís of India and Burma, *Living the Life*, pp. 19-20.
208 Written on behalf of Shoghi Effendi, letter dated 7 July 1944 to an individual, ibid., p. 21.
209 Written on behalf of Shoghi Effendi, letter dated 17 October 1944 to an individual, ibid., p. 21.
210 Written on behalf of Shoghi Effendi, letter dated 13 May 1945 to an individual, ibid., p. 23.
211 Written on behalf of Shoghi Effendi, letter dated 20 March 1946 to the National Spiritual Assembly of the United States and Canada, *Lights of Guidance; A Bahá'í Reference File*, comp. Helen Hornby, rev. ed. (New Delhi: Bahá'í Publishing Trust, 1988) p. 404.
212 Written on behalf of Shoghi Effendi, letter dated 5 September 1946 to an individual, *Living the Life*, p. 25.
213 Letter dated 19 September 1948 to an individual, ibid., p. 29.
214 Written on behalf of Shoghi Effendi, letter dated 30 September 1949 to an individual, ibid., pp. 30-1.
215 Written on behalf of Shoghi Effendi, letter dated 12 October 1949 to an individual, ibid., p. 403.
216 Letter dated 24 February 1950 to an individual, ibid., p. 32.
217 Written on behalf of Shoghi Effendi, letter dated 4 October 1950 to an individual, ibid., p. 32.
218 Written on behalf of Shoghi Effendi, letter dated 4 October 1950 to an individual, ibid., pp. 32-3.
219 Written on behalf of Shoghi Effendi, letter dated 5 October 1950 to an individual, ibid., p. 33.
220 Written on behalf of Shoghi Effendi, letter dated 18 December 1945 to an individual, ibid., p. 24.
221 Written on behalf of the Universal House of Justice, letter dated 30 August 1982 to individuals in Africa.

Chapter 12

222 Bahá'u'lláh, *Kitáb-i-Íqán; The Book of Certitude*, trans. Shoghi Effendi, 3rd ed. (London: Bahá'í Publishing Trust, 1982) pp. 123-4.
223 Bahá'u'lláh, *The Hidden Words*, p. 11.
224 Bahá'u'lláh, ibid.
225 Bahá'u'lláh, ibid., p. 65.
226 Bahá'u'lláh, ibid., p. 80.
227 'Abdu'l-Bahá, *Star of the West*, vol. 4, no. 11, 27 September 1913, p. 192.
228 Written on behalf of Shoghi Effendi, letter dated 11 February 1925 to the National Spiritual Assembly National Spiritual Assembly of the British Isles, *Lights of Guidance*, p. 88.
229 Written on behalf of Shoghi Effendi, letter dated 11 February 1925 to the National Spiritual Assembly National Spiritual Assembly of the British Isles, followed by an extract from the Guardian's postscript, ibid., p. 89.
230 Written on behalf of Shoghi Effendi, letter dated 11 February 1925 to the National Spiritual Assembly National Spiritual Assembly of the British Isles, ibid., p. 94.
231 Written on behalf of Shoghi Effendi, letter dated 12 May 1925 to an individual, *Living the Life*, p. 10.
232 Written on behalf of Shoghi Effendi, letter dated 11 January 1950 to an individual, *Lights of Guidance*, p. 90.
233 Written on behalf of Shoghi Effendi, letter dated 16 February 1951 to an individual, *Living the Life*, pp. 33-4.
234 Written on behalf of Shoghi Effendi, letter dated 23 September 1975 to an individual, *Lights of Guidance*, pp. 90-1.
235 Written on behalf of Shoghi Effendi, letter dated 13 August 1980, ibid., pp. 89-90.

Chapter 13

236 Bahá'u'lláh, *Gleanings*, CXLVI, pp. 314-15.
237 'Abdu'l-Bahá, *Selections*, 193, pp. 229-31.
238 'Abdu'l-Bahá, *Paris Talks*, p. 123.
239 'Abdu'l-Bahá, quoted in Shoghi Effendi and Lady Blomfield, *The Ascension of 'Abdu'l-Bahá* (London: Bahá'í Publishing Trust, n.d.) pp. 27-8.

INDEX

'Abdu'l-Bahá ('the Master'), 184, 192, 194, 196, 202, 212, 215, 216, 220, 228, 231, 234, 235, 237, 239
Abhá Paradise, 110, 133
accord, 113
Adam, 6, 47, 74
affection, 42, 105, 178
affinity, 41
Age, this enlightened, wondrous, 9, 58, 59, 92
agreement, 143, 178, 186
aggression, 91, 93
anarchy, 10
angels, 133, 158, 239
animosity, 37, 142
antagonism, 188
association, 37, 38, 68
attachment, 217
attraction, 33, 34, 35, 38
aversion, 111
autonomy, national, 94, 98

Báb, 182, 216, 231
backbiting, 222-31, 234-5, 237
Bahá'í Faith ('the Cause'; 'the Cause of God'; 'the Cause of the Ancient Beauty'; 'the Faith'; 'the Faith of Bahá'u'lláh', 'the Faith of God', 'His Cause'; 'the Holy Faith'; 'the religion of God'; 'this sacred Dispensation'), 91, 105, 126, 163, 175, 203, 209, 221, 237, 239
   administrative order, 125, 161, 162, 206, 216, 219
   Central Figures (Founders), 186, 203
   expansion (growth, progress), 128, 160, 162, 202, 204, 206, 210
   golden age, 30
   institutions, 128, 204
   integrity, 160, 164
   interests, 197, 229, 234
   laws, 125, 168
   mission, divine, 203
   principles, 125, 198
   promotion (propagation), 107, 200, 237
   purpose (goal), 99, 104, 161, 198
   should not become source of discord, hate, enmity, 104
   spirit of, 49, 148, 202, 216
   teachings, 125, 148, 164, 168, 173, 174, 214, 219, 229, 232
   unity, 112, 152, 160, 164
Bahá'ís ('Bahá'í community'; 'believers'; 'beloved of the Lord'; 'children of the Kingdom'; 'friends'; 'friends of God'; 'loved ones of God'; 'lovers of God'; 'people of Bahá'; 'people of God'; 'people of Justice'), 106, 108, 109, 128, 151, 185
   anger among, 123, 234
   apathy among, 200
   conflict, contention among, 179, 188, 237, 200, 201
   criticism among, 161, 233, 234

deeds (acts), 108, 115, 118, 140, 144, 179
differences, discord, dissension, dispute among, 188, 200, 201, 202, 221, 236
dissidence, 161
disunity, inharmony among, 210, 229, 233
distinction, 115
diversity, 151
enemies, 135
estrangement among, 200
example, 147, 215, 235, 236
fellowship, 107, 190
hearts, 124, 132
immaturity, 205, 209
labours, 107
martyrs, 149, 216
misdeeds, 234
misunderstanding, 233
model for study, 151
objective, 161
one spiritual family, 146
persecution, 149, 163
pioneers, 221
power, 148
purpose, 125
qualities required of,
   accord, 115, 116, 117
   affection, 179
   agreement, 120, 124
   amity, 201, 236, 239
   attraction to Divine Fragrances, 189
   candour, 192
   care, 191
   character, praiseworthy, 108
   cheer, 135
   concord, 236, 239
   conduct, excellence of, 166
   cooperation, 202, 232
   ourage, 221
   courtesy, 191
   dedication, 211
   detachment, 144, 189, 202
   devotion, 148, 191
   dignity, 191
   effort, 203, 215
   encourage (praise) fellow believers, 197
   faithfulness, 115, 141
   fellowship, 129, 221, 236, 239
   firmness, 115
   forbearance toward each other, 204, 234
   forgiveness, 123, 219, 221, 234

123

friendliness, 129, 236
friendship, 135, 138
goodness, 236
good-will, 141
harmony, 121, 148, 187, 209, 210, 213, 216, 221, 239
honesty of purpose, 192
humility, 118, 189, 221
joy, 148
justice, 115
kindness, 134, 135, 236
kindliness, 136, 141
kinship, spiritual, 205
long-suffering in face of difficulties, 189
love, 115, 131, 138, 139, 147, 216, 239
    between husband and wife, 166
    for each other, 113, 116, 120, 126, 179, 190, 197, 201, 206, 207, 209, 210, 211, 213, 215, 219, 221, 235
    for God, 122
    for humanity, 115, 135, 136, 142, 215
lowliness, 189
luminous, 144
mercy, 144, 197, 234
moderation, 191
modesty, 118
morals, 115
patience, 189, 194, 197, 204, 206, 234, 235
peace, 119
perseverance, 221
praise one another, 197, 237
prayerful, 211, 215
promoting international peace, 115
purity of motive, 189, 197, 202, 221
radiance, 148, 197
removing prejudices, 115, 121
restraint, 194
sanctity, 117
self-sacrificing, 139, 206, 212, 216, 236
selflessness, 135, 148, 202
service, 202
    spirit of, 215
    to the Bahá'í Faith, 202
    to the human world, 115
servitude to His exalted Threshold, 189
signs and tokens of God's great mercy, 136
sin-covering eye, 219
sincerity, 115, 239
singleness of mind, 192
solidarity, spiritual, 183
spiritual, 144
    development, 118
    strength, 206, 235
steadfastness, 115
tenderness, 135

truthfulness, 141, 239
understanding, 206, 210, 235
union, 114, 116
unity, 106, 115, 117, 118, 119, 120, 121, 122, 123, 147, 148, 153, 154, 183, 187, 197, 199, 202, 205, 20, 211, 216, 219, 221, 231, 235, 236, 239
    of thought and action, 202
uprightness, 141, 236
vigilance, 203
warmth, 146
wisdom, 221
quarrelling among, 216
relationships, 210
shortcomings, 204, 234
souls, 124
strife among, 200
task, 150
tests, 205, 214, 220
thoughts, 118
work, 148
Bahá'u'lláh, 67, 76, 87, 88, 89, 90, 96, 98, 99, 125, 128, 167, 168, 182, 197, 207, 228, 231
aim, purpose, 86, 116, 175
belief in, 163
good pleasure, 236
grace, 141
Law of, 94
love for, 213
loyalty to, 203
Messenger of God, 163
might, 92
mission, 101
Order of, 102, 103
Revelation, 28, 101, 103, 152, 160
    goal, 101
    principle, 101
statutes, 83
sufferings, 103
Tablets, 101
teachings, 48, 95, 114, 126
titles:–
    the All-Bountiful, 236
    the Ancient Beauty, 92, 103, 237
    the Blessed Beauty, 237
    the Blessed Perfection, 116
    the Faithful, 236
    the Gracious, 236
    the Lord of Hosts, 158
    the Most Great Name, 92, 132
    the Most High, 236
    the Pen of the Most High, 82, 85
    blessed Perfection, 120
    the Temple of God amongst men, 236

   this Wronged One, 108
   Truth of, 126
   verses, 85, 101
   vision, 151
   Word, 85, 120, 237
   words, 82
   world order, 160, 185, 203
benevolence, 179
bigotry, religious, 77
blessings, Divine, 191
bliss, 177
body politic, 41
bonds, spiritual, 93
Books (heavenly, holy), 55, 75, 83, 163
borders, boundaries, 23, 47
brotherhood, 36, 68, 70, 72, 75, 77, 95, 163
Burning Bush, 131

centralization, 94
character, 45
   diversity of, 60
children, 12, 168
Christ, 76
city state, unity of, 10
civilization, material, 11
   new, 185
class, 98, 125, 151
colour, 43, 44, 45, 125
Company on high, 133
concord, 83, 105, 130, 182, 184
confirmation, Divine, 191
conflict, 86, 91, 93, 108
confusion, 109
consultation, 151, 175, 190, 196
contention, 19, 86, 91, 108, 142
convictions, diversity of, 61
conviviality, 186
cooperation, 37, 72, 182
corruption, 51, 199
Counsellors, 234
country, 65
   love of one's, 4
courtesy, 186
Covenant, 93, 103, 152-64, 237, 239
   firmness in, 155
   power of, 153, 156, 157, 159
creation, 102, 123
creed, 98, 125
cultures, 151
cursing (reviling), 86, 106
customs, difference of, 60

death, 33, 34, 35, 38, 41

deeds (actions), 18, 105, 133, 163
demilitarization, 31, 95
denominations, 88
dependence, 36
depression, 234
desire, 122, 199
detachment, 18
devotion, 72
dignity, 51
discord, 17, 35, 76, 109, 189
disappointment, 40
dispute, 27
dissension, 40, 93, 104, 107
disunity, 34, 100
divorce, 166, 168, 172, 174

East, 29, 88
ecumenism, 12
education, 9
ego, 221
elderly, 135
emotionalism, 95
enemies, 89, 91
enlightenment, 183
enmity, 88, 109, 131, 141, 171
equality, 144
estrangement, 141, 191
ethnical origins, diversity, 94
excellence, 45

faith, 173
faithfulness, 130
family, 168-75
   agreement, 171
   love, 171
   unity, 10, 170, 175
fanaticism, 77
fault-finding, 223-6, 229-31, 235
federalism, world, 29, 31, 95
fellowship (comradeship), 41, 55, 57, 64, 68, 73, 76, 85, 93, 104, 134, 178, 179, 182, 186
finance, 31, 95
force, 29
forgiveness, 208
fraternity, 75
free will, 163
freedom, 103
   of expression, 189, 191
   personal, 98
friendliness, friendship, 85, 186, 238

God, 19, 20, 23, 29, 43, 52, 57, 64, 65, 81, 84, 109, 112, 128, 142, 176, 179, 180, 189, 195, 196, 211, 216, 217, 221, 233

125

aid, 200
attributes, 65
   beauty, 93, 113, 237
   glory, 80
   grace, 5, 59, 84, 91, 138, 145
   grandeur, 123
   kindness, 84, 88, 106
   love, 145, 163
   mercy, 5, 88, 90, 136
   might, 110
   nurturing, 88
   oneness, 74, 88, 114
   power, 59, 78, 96, 110, 200
   sovereignty, 86, 163, 200
   will, 26, 53, 58, 132, 162, 197, 221
   wrath, 90
bestowals, 145
Book of, 86
bounties, 26, 143, 237
call, 76
command, 23, 26, 221
commandments, 134
confirmation, 110
Day of, 107
favours, 84
gift of, 58
good pleasure, 143
inspiration of, 3
instructions, 135
is love, 26
knowledge of, 55, 113
law of, 201
love of, 46, 80, 88, 93, 106, 115, 123, 144, 208, 215, 218
ordinances, 101
path of, 86, 217
plan, 150
presence, 187
protection of, 5, 88
purpose, 197
recognition of, 105
sign of, 59, 110, 123
teachings, 114, 145
titles:–
   the All-glorious, 93
   the All-Knowing, 200
   the All-Wise, 200
   the Almighty, 5, 197
   Creator, 2, 90, 123, 163, 168
   the Eternal Truth, 132, 200
   Father, 89, 218
   the Great, 86
   the Highest, 144
   Incomparable, 2
   the Lord, 76, 145, 189, 237
     of mankind, 75
     of might, 86
     of strength, 86
     of unity, 23
   the Mighty, 86
   Shepherd, 145
   the Sun of Reality, 77
   the Unifier, 200
   Unknowable Essence, 163
trust in, 86, 222
Word of, 42, 48, 59, 61, 62, 92, 93, 160
world of, 76, 123
goodwill, 163
gossip, 232
governments, 9
greed, 202

habits, 60
   diversity, 94
happiness, 120
harmony, 34, 35, 121, 166, 167, 174, 191, 195
   law of, 33
   spiritual, 79
harshness, 59
hate, hatred, 27, 35, 37, 59, 109, 131, 132, 141, 171, 188, 215, 221
   thoughts of, 22
hearts, 87, 89, 93, 94, 106, 109, 119, 121, 122, 125, 142, 147, 157, 176, 179, 182, 183, 200, 207, 217, 237
   attraction of, 146, 180
   thoughts of, 22
helpfulness, 36
Hidden Words
history, 24, 940
holiness, 138
Holy Spirit, 48, 67, 68, 70, 71, 72, 75, 191
home, 168, 173
hospitality, 186
hostility, 59
human nature, 213
human race ('children of men'; 'the human kingdom'; 'humankind'; 'man'; 'mankind'; 'men'; 'peoples and kindreds of the earth'; 'people of the world'; 'world of humanity'), 1, 2, 146
   accomplishment, 57
   advancement, 73
   affinity, 41
   agreement, 46, 70, 77, 75, 116
   all created by God, 2, 47, 88, 218
   all embody divine possibilities, 44
   amity among, 21
   association among, with, 16, 130
   attraction, 33
   beauty of, 41

blending of, 41
children of God, 139
coming of age, 151
common properties, 46
concord, 53
cooperation, 57
coordination, 71
destiny, 28
differences among, 6, 84, 88
dissension among, 40, 85, 132
distinctions, 46
disunion, 46
disunity, disunion, division, 32, 38, 46, 54, 85
diversity, 11, 31
enlightenment, 67, 73
equality, 8
evolution of, 10, 30, 96
fellowship, 55, 76
glory of, 7, 72
God makes no distinction between, 5, 44
happiness of, 21
harassed, 10
harmony, 21, 33
heritage, 7
ills, 100
interdependence, 9
interests, 104
in image of God, 44
love among, 21, 73, 74, 76, 104
love for, 4
maturity, 10
not perfect, 123
one family, 57, 89
oneness, 11, 51, 58, 90, 95, 96, 101, 145, 149, 156, 163, 164, 178
peace, 82, 100
physical relationship, 36
quickening, spiritual, 67
redemption, 73
rights, 8
security, 82, 100
servants (subjects) of one God, 3, 43, 88
solidarity, 46
tranquillity, 132
unification, 10, 28, 86, 93, 100, 150
unity, 9, 21, 31, 33, 41, 46, 52, 53, 55, 65, 70, 71, 73, 74, 76, 77, 82, 87, 88, 89, 97, 98, 99, 100, 104, 114, 116, 149, 151, 161, 198
weakness, 46
well-being, 82, 100, 132

ideals, 174
ideas, diversity of, 60, 61
identities, multiple, 122
ignorance, 26, 95, 141

ill-feeling, 189
illumination, 171, 180
illusion, 47
imagination, 26, 63, 106
imitations, 77
impatience, 123
inharmony, 34, 187
initiative, individual, 98
injustice, 59
institutions, 94
interests, earthly, 68
Iran, 149, 162, 163

joy, 103, 178, 185
justice, 29, 160

kindliness, 91, 132
kindness, 72, 75
Kingdom, 76, 120, 133, 158
   of Bahá, 189, 239
   of God, 166
      on earth, 150, 160, 163
      on High, 191
Kitáb-i-Aqdas, 182
Kitáb-i-Íqán, 221
knowledge, 110

language, diversity, 94
   unity of, 20, 31, 95
learning, 110
Lesser Peace, 150
liberty, 103
life, 33, 35, 38, 39, 40, 41, 101, 145
   eternal, everlasting, 76, 150
limitations, 91
love, 23, 26, 33, 35, 57, 74, 75, 85, 89, 91, 93, 132, 133, 146, 167, 171, 174, 177, 180, 182, 183, 190, 191, 215, 232
   infinite, 65
   thoughts of, 22
loving kindness, 91
loyalty, 94

malevolence, 59
malice, 17, 83
manners, 60
marriage, 165-9
mercy, 123
minds, 41, 107, 157, 180
   varying types, 79
mischief, 83
misery, 40
morals, 115
Most Great Peace, 58, 150, 160

mysteries, divine, 182
nations, 10, 32, 58, 64, 65, 74, 77, 88, 89, 98, 101, 121, 142, 151
    accord, 41
    cooperation, 95
    differences, 66
    disunity, 32
    diversity, 94
    interdependence, 28
    regeneration, 130
    unity, 10, 41
nationalities, 77
nature, examples from, 33, 34, 35, 40, 59
Nineteen Day Feast, 176-86
nineteenth century, 100

opinions, 190, 195
    clash of, 189, 193
    diversity, 60, 79
oneness, 39, 54, 79, 93, 138143, 166
order, 56, 109
otherness, 137
parents, 168
passion, 122, 167, 217
patience, 86, 208
patriotism, 94
peace, 41, 51, 56, 64, 74, 84, 100, 103, 121, 145, 238
    thoughts of, 22
peoples, 64, 74, 87, 88, 89, 92, 95, 151,
perfection, 123
    human, 60
politics, 31, 65
prejudice, 11, 23, 24, 25, 46, 50, 63, 66, 128
    age, 128
    class, 11, 128
    colour, 11
    cultural, 128
    economic, 128
    educational, 11, 128
    national, 11, 128
    patriotic, 24
    political, 128, 142
    racial, 11, 24, 47, 64, 128, 142
    religious (creed), 11, 24, 128, 142
    tribal, 128
prayer, 196, 197, 238
progress, 37, 51, 100, 101, 102, 103, 170, 185
Prophets of God ('Divine Manifestations'; 'Divine Messengers'; 'Manifestations of the Word'), 54, 55, 57, 62, 74, 75, 76, 77, 95, 152
purity, 133
    of motive, 191

race, 3, 44
races, 88. 98, 140
    accord between, 41
    discrimination, 49
    diversity, 94
    enmity between, 48
    equality, 46
    fellowship, 46
    harmony, 48
    hatred between, 48
    inequality, 46
    no difference in sight of God, 47
    unity, 41, 42, 43
racism, 51
rancour, 141
Realm of Glory, 191
rectitude of conduct, 91
relationships, 93
religion, 3, 9, 53, 56, 57, 73, 81, 145
    religions (revelations, dispensations), 12, 16, 79, 85, 90, 119, 121, 134, 140, 141, 164, 208
    oneness, 58, 77
    reconciliation, 142
    unity, 57, 63, 64
remorse, 166
remoteness, 38
repulsion, 35, 38
resources, 29
ruin, 37, 40

sanctity, 133
sciences, 11, 115
sects, 88
selfishness, 202
sentiments, diversity of, 61
separation, 33, 35
service, 186
Shoghi Effendi ('the beloved Guardian'), 149, 175, 196, 206, 208, 209, 235
sincerity, 91, 130
society, 163, 168, 172, 182, 185
souls, 41, 69, 77, 87, 93, 113, 121, 122, 123, 158, 163, 237
sovereigns, 20
Spiritual Assemblies ('councils'), 187-98
    local, 192, 210, 219, 229, 234
    national, 192, 210, 229, 234
spirits, unity of, 113
state sovereignty, 10
strangers, 91, 136
strength, 87
strife, 23, 27, 83, 88, 107
superstition, 47, 77
Supreme Concourse, 180

talk, idle, 222
temperament, diversity of, 60

thought, thoughts, 22, 27, 60, 61, 94, 180
trade, 9, 31, 95
traditions, diversity, 94
transformation, 148
tranquillity, 170
tribes, 10, 64, 74
truth, 25, 27, 63, 66, 77, 78, 123, 189, 190, 191, 194, 237
twentieth century, 12

understanding, 83, 89
uniformity, 94
union, 109, 161, 166, 239
unity, 13, 14, 15, 17, 18, 19, 26, 28, 33, 34, 38, 40, 53, 82, 83, 84, 113, 130, 144, 150, 151, 169, 174, 177, 184, 185, 186, 190, 238
    Divine, 93
    in diversity, 94
    in the home, 173
    thoughts of, 22
Universal House of Justice, 221, 229, 234, 235
universality, 91

virtues, 76, 107, 110

want, 103
war, 12, 23, 24, 29, 47, 58, 68, 77, 88, 103, 145, 238
    thoughts of, 22
weakness, 46
wealth, 115
West, 29
wickedness, 76
will, 102
wisdom, 183
world, 94
    citizenship, 30
    civilization, 30
    commonwealth, 98
    community, 29
    culture, 30
    healing, 81
    leaders, 28
    order, 11
    redemption of, 236
    unity, 10, 12, 63, 150, 186

youth, 12, 135, 168

Biographical Notes

Bahá'u'lláh (1817-1892) Founder of the Bahá'í Faith, Who proclaimed that the human race is on the verge of attaining its long awaited maturity, a condition prophesied of old as the Kingdom of God on earth. Bahá'u'lláh's challenging claim is that He is the Messenger of God to this new age, sent to guide humanity through the troubled times it now faces. Imprisoned and persecuted for His teachings by the religious and civil authorities of His day, Bahá'u'lláh endured 40 years of exile from His native Persia, and finally passed away at Bahjí, just outside 'Akká, in the Holy Land. His resting place is visited by thousands of Bahá'ís every year from around the world as an act of pilgrimage. His Writings, which number over a hundred volumes, encompass virtually every aspect of human experience. These Writings, along with those of the Báb, are considered by Bahá'ís to be the revealed Word of God.

The Báb (1819-1850) Prophet and herald of the coming of Bahá'u'lláh. His Writings, along with those of Bahá'u'lláh, are considered by Bahá'ís to be the revealed Word of God. The Báb's teachings of the advent of a new Revelation were received with violent opposition from the rulers of Persia, who eventually had Him publicly executed. His shrine, on the slopes of Mount Carmel in the Holy Land, has become famed for its beauty, and is known as the 'Queen of Carmel'.

'Abdu'l-Bahá (1844-1921) Eldest son of Bahá'u'lláh, appointed by Him 'Centre of the Covenant'. Having endured imprisonment and exile with His father from an early age, 'Abdu'l-Bahá was freed in 1908. Shortly thereafter He set out to spread news of Bahá'u'lláh's teachings in Egypt, Europe and North America, where He was widely acclaimed as the 'Prophet of Peace'.

Shoghi Effendi (1897-1957) Grandson of 'Abdu'l-Bahá, appointed by Him Guardian and World Head of the Bahá'í Faith in His Will and Testament. From 1921 until his own passing, Shoghi Effendi dedicated himself to firmly establishing the Bahá'í administrative order, to providing authoritative translations of the Bahá'í sacred Writings, and to moulding the diverse followers of Bahá'u'lláh into a single, world-wide community, conscious of its own identity and unity.

The Universal House of Justice (first elected 1963) Ordained by Bahá'u'lláh in His Most Holy Book, this institution now stands as the central authority of the Bahá'í Faith. Its nine members are elected at an international convention every five years by members of all Bahá'í National Spiritual Assemblies throughout the world (currently 165 in number).

Further Reading

GLEANINGS FROM THE WRITINGS OF BAHÁ'U'LLÁH
A collection of the most characteristic passages from outstanding works revealed throughout Bahá'u'lláh's 40-year ministry, illustrating major themes in His Writings, including the greatness of this day; the unity of God; God's creation; the Most Great Peace; the qualities of the true seeker. A representative selection of the sacred writings of the Author of the Bahá'í Revelation, compiled and translated by Shoghi Effendi.
Bahá'í Publishing Trust: London
cloth; 350 pp; 22 x 14 cm; 0-900125-38-1; £7.95

THE HIDDEN WORDS
Bahá'u'lláh
One of Bahá'u'lláh's most popular works, composed of brief and stirring epigrams – verses of guidance and comfort, which convey the essence of all religions: God's eternal love for humanity, and His desire that we should live at peace with each other on His earth. Bahá'u'lláh described The Hidden Words as 'the inner essence' of the wisdom of the Prophets of old, 'clothed in the garment of brevity'. A guide to living for millions around the globe, this book forms the ethical heart of Bahá'u'lláh's message.
Nightingale Books, London
paper; 104 pp; 17 x 13cm; illustrated; 0-900125-93-4; £5.95

MEDITATIONS OF THE BLESSED BEAUTY
Bahá'u'lláh
A selection of some of Bahá'u'lláh's most powerful writings on the themes of creation and spiritual regeneration. These inspirational words reveal a creative force which is truly awe-inspiring and magnificent in scope, drawing the reader into a contemplation of that mysterious power which binds each of us to the cosmos. these exquisite verses will attract the hearts of all seekers after truth and beauty. Complemented by a specially commissioned set of photographs which explore the profound symbolism of physical creation.
Nightingale Books, London
96 pp; 23 x 21 cm; illustrated
cloth; 1-870989-17-1; £17.95
paper; 1-870989-18-X; £9.95

THE PROMISE OF WORLD PEACE
The Universal House of Justice
The Bahá'í International Community was honoured with a 'Peace Messenger' award by the United Nations for the publication and dissemination of this statement, which presents a powerful argument for change to a peaceful, cooperative global society.
Bahá'í Publishing Trust, Wilmette, IL
paper; 40 pp; 23 x 18 cm; 0-900125-68-3; £2.50

THE POWER OF UNITY; BEYOND PREJUDICE AND RACISM
Bahá'u'lláh, the Báb, 'Abdu'l-Bahá, Shoghi Effendi, the Universal House of Justice
A comprehensive selection of extracts from the Bahá'í writings on the issue of prejudice, the elimination of which Bahá'ís identify as one of the most important aspects of the peace process. Addresses such issues as: the rights of minorities; education for the abolition of prejudice; interracial marriage; unity in diversity.
Bahá'í Publishing Trust, Wilmettte, IL
paper; 156 pp; 22 x 14 cm; no ISBN; £6.95

BAHÁ'U'LLÁH
Bahá'í International Community, Office of Public Information
The definitive presentation of the life and teachings of Bahá'u'lláh, founder of the Bahá'í Faith. Explains the station and mission of Bahá'u'lláh in clear and challenging terms, summarizes his most important teachings, and expresses his claims to fulfil the prophetic hopes of all religions. Includes an extensive glossary, defining unfamiliar terms and concepts, and providing background information on people, places and events mentioned in the text.
Bahá'í Publications, Mona Vale, NSW
112 pp; illustrated
cloth; 22 x 15 cm; 0-909991-53-7; £5.95
paper; 18 x 11 cm; 0-909991-51-0; £2.50

THE BAHÁ'ÍS; A PROFILE OF THE BAHÁ'Í FAITH AND ITS WORLDWIDE COMMUNITY
Bahá'í International Community, Office of Public Information
A magazine-format publication, specially designed for people who need to have accurate and up-to-date information at their fingertips. A rich variety of colour photographs, charts and diagrams illustrate the origin, development, current state and future prospects of the Bahá'í community around the glob, as well as presenting a satisfying overview of the main beliefs, practices and goals of the Bahá'í Faith.
Bahá'í Publishing Trust, London
paper; 80 pp; 28 x 21 cm; illustrated; 1-870989-37-6; £2.50

EMERGENCE; DIMENSIONS OF A NEW WORLD ORDER
Charles Lerche (ed)
Six essays by Bahá'í working in the fields of conflict resolution, development studies, law, economics, history and ecology consider the meaning of 'world order' from a variety of standpoints, and present the distinctive elements of the Bahá'í model as a sign of hope for our collective future.
Bahá'í Publishing Trust, London
paper; 192 pp; 21 x 14 cm; 1-870989-22-8; £6.95

The Bahá'í Faith

In just over 150 years, the Bahá'í Faith has grown from an obscure movement in the Middle East to the second-most geographically widespread of the independent world religions (*according to the 1992 Britannica Book of the Year*). Embracing people from more than 2100 ethnic, racial and tribal groups, it is quite likely the most diverse organized body of people on the planet. Its unity challenges prevailing theories about human nature and the prospects for our common future.

The Bahá'í Faith has no priesthood; its affairs are administered by elected councils at local, national and international level. Bahá'ís all over the world work together in service to humanity by furthering the principles of their Faith, which include: the unity of the human race; the strengthening of family life; the equality of the sexes; universal education; social and economic development; harmonization of science and religion; the elimination of extremes of wealth and poverty; protection of the environment; eradication of all forms of prejudice; and the establishment of a just and peaceful social order in which the rights of all peoples are fully recognized and protected.